KLEZMER for the JOYFUL SOUL

Debbie Burke

KLEZMER FOR THE JOYFUL SOUL
By Debbie Burke

Maiden, maiden tell me again
What can grow, grow without rain,
What can burn for many years,
What can long and cry without tears?

Silly young lad, why ask again?
It's a stone that can grow, grow without rain,
It's love that can burn for many long years,
A heart that can yearn and cry without tears.

"Tumbalalaika"
Russian Jewish folk song
Date unknown

Dreams and Wishes
Most often come true
When the Mind and the Heart
Are joined with Faith.

James L. Thompson, Jr.
Paper Orphans © 2007

Dedicated to Sarah Lehrer, the grandmother I never knew. Maybe somehow this will bridge the gap.

Also by Debbie Burke

"The Poconos in B Flat"
"Glissando – A Story of Love, Lust and Jazz"
"Tasty Jazz Jams for Our Times (Vol. 1)"
"Tasty Jazz Jams for Our Times (Vol. 2)"
"Music in the Scriptures"
"Icarus Flies Home"

FOREWORD

While some dismiss musical revivals as backwards-looking, Hill and Bithell(1) note that to find success these movements require the hard work of visionary creators. Dreaming of a better world with music at its center, these activists may be involved in a number of efforts-- researching and often reimagining history, creating new venues and contexts for performances, developing educational resources, and promoting the work of important artists. And, of course, there is the required investment of long hours to produce a refined and rooted musical sound.

Starting in the mid-1970s as a small blip on the Jewish cultural radar of the US's East and West Coasts, the revitalization of klezmer and the wider Yiddish culture is now a fully-fledged global movement in its fifth decade. Today, thousands of artists and activists around the world have made the advancement of Yiddish their life's mission.

Klezmer is both an art and a functional practice-- the music has an important place in Jewish communities as a soundtrack for weddings, *bar/bat mitzvahs* and other community celebrations. Additionally, it offers a beautiful expressivity fit for major concert halls, steeped in echoes of the synagogue and Yiddish sensibility.

For many in the contemporary scene, their work is about expanding Jewish identity into the realm of arts/culture/aesthetics, in opposition to the currents of mainstream Judaism which frame Jewish identity principally in religious terms, or posit it in reference to assumed support for the Israeli state. So, the Yiddish revival can be seen as part of reclaiming and inventing a more holistic idea of a distinctive peoplehood.

Debbie Burke's book is a much-needed addition to the growing library of writings on the topic, uniquely providing first-hand testimonies from a diverse range of today's Yiddish cultural heroes. Their voices will take you behind the curtain of contemporary klezmer stages to understand the impulses and motivations propelling an international effort to revitalize some of the Jewish world's greatest treasures.

Mit a hartsikn dank,
Pete Rushefsky
Center for Traditional Music and Dance & Yiddish New York
2021

1. Juniper Hill and Caroline Bithell, The Oxford Handbook of Musical Revival (Oxford University Press, 2014).

AUTHOR'S NOTES

When I looked at the genealogy study that my uncle sent to me in 1998, a few stunning things came to light about the towns my forebears lived in, their ultimate extraordinary passage to America and their hardships once they got here (in my case, taking them to the Lower East Side of Manhattan). Their ebullience to be on American shores was blemished by experiencing abject poverty, alcoholism, business failure, infidelity and general existential malaise. With all that, I have to believe that some new joys occasionally infiltrated their lives in the form of music. Somewhere in the air, there was music: Yiddish music, Yiddish theater and klezmer.

The body of work that coalesced to become klezmer was informed by suffering and pain, joy and mirth, and the disjointed paths they and thousands of others followed that eventually led them to settle in the US.

The music of my heritage was gingerly laced through my past experiences. I heard strains of it in my early grade-school years through the occasional Yiddish song fragments sung by my maternal grandmother and through the music I heard during a handful of visits to synagogue. The cantors always had beautiful, rich voices that could bend a note better than I ever could on alto sax. Known for its plaintive, imploring quality, a singing cry, the sound of it, I admit – with all of its tragedy, the leadenness and the soaring, searing heights of it – was, actually embarrassing to me, so I avoided listening to it.

I've written avidly and hungrily about jazz since 2016. Sometimes, I'd come across klezmer musicians. I'd listen to them on YouTube, read their bios and, when I interviewed them, I paused to consider what their responses conveyed between the lines. Slowly, I found myself mentally bookmarking this music. It became something to come back to, something to explore once I 'had the time.' Klezmer had a primal feel to it that made those family photo albums come to life. Its modes, chords, instrumentation and thick textures combined into an artform that begged a second look.

For over six decades, I've resisted the pull to learn more about the building blocks of this music and the heart that beats inside of it. With all its demands and emotions, I'd stopped it from seeping in. I'd wallowed in my embarrassment over feeling too deeply.

Until now.

Part I of this book presents a brief and informal history of klezmer music with much help from ethnomusicologists, historians, authors and people of faith. Part II uses a Q&A format to appreciate klezmer's soul through the eyes of the music community.

I hope you enjoy this book and that you find your own journey with the music. Even if it does not reflect your own family's path, there is a great enlightenment that comes with finding out what happens behind the notes in any deeply rooted genre. The people and their stories are behind the music.

Debbie Burke

Debbie Burke

PART I – Klezmer in Context

WHEN DID IT START: THE WAVES

Born in The Pale of Settlement approximately 700 years ago and influenced by the music surrounding it from the Ottoman Empire and for example by Balkan music, klezmer has enjoyed several "waves" or rebirths: a revival in the 1970s, a subsequent second wave from the 1980s into the 1990s, and then what is now known as the third generation.

Although derived from cantorial music(2), is it insular; did it evolve according to the faith of its founders and followers, and then, has it only been consumed by these same groups? Musicologist Dr. David Hebert says the appeal is wide, and he points to a similar pattern for many types of music. "This is a common phenomenon seen in most kinds of religious music worldwide. As life in general is increasingly secularized, music experiences a similar process (see my book Music Glocalization: Heritage and Innovation in a Digital Age). Most people don't think of reggae as religious music, but it originally was intimately connected with Rastafarianism in Jamaica. Many popular Christmas songs were actually written by Jewish composers, which also indicates something about religious rituals as an opportunity for musicians, rather than necessarily always requiring a particular theological stance. Much of the European choral tradition is based on texts with strong religious connotations, but across time, styles are modified and the connotations shift to become more open to performance in secular contexts."

The old television ad "You don't have to be Jewish to love Levy's Rye" can be re-stated in terms of who loves and appreciates klezmer today. Says Prof. Hebert, "While klezmer is clearly connected to Jewish and Jewish-American heritage, its sounds can be deeply meaningful for all people." Dr. Douglas Kiman, an ethnomusicologist and clarinetist, says, "I think that most people are attracted to klezmer for its ties with cultural Judaism. Jews can reconnect with their cultural roots without religion to religion or Israel, and non-Jews can connect to Jewish culture through klezmer as an easy gateway."

[2] Cantorial music developed first; it is the chanting of the Torah, a 3000-year-old tradition. Klezmer emerged about 600 years ago. While cantorial music, also known as *khazonos*, has lyrics, klezmer in its original state was purely instrumental. Through subsequent waves as it has evolved in the US and elsewhere, klezmer songs have included lyrics, often sung in Yiddish.

SONGS and BANDS

Broadly speaking, there are categories of songs within klezmer, such as a "doina" (according to Wikipedia, a Romanian musical style possibly with Middle Eastern roots); a "hora" (a Romanian or Israeli dance style in which participants and performers form a ring); and a "bulgar" or "freylekh" (music of merriment and pleasure). To add yet another layer to it, several new genres have now splintered off to create what Kiman calls "hybridities": Klunk (klezmer punk); Anakronic Electro Orkestra ("electro-Yiddish with a little bit of klezmer"); and klezmer combined with either experimental music, groove-funk, rock or jazz.

A smattering of specific songs important for any beginner to know include both the serious and the jovial, such as:

The Khaneke (Chanukah) song "Drey Dreydl," sung notably by New York City cantor Moishe Oysher (1906-1958).

"Echad Me Yodea?" ("Who Knows One"), a song that invites - some say requires - participation as the stanzas count off *who knows one* (God); two (the tablets of the covenant); three (the patriarchs); four (the matriarchs); up through thirteen (the attributes of God).

The powerful and stirring "Ono Hashem" ("Please God/I am Your Servant") from Psalms 116:16.

"Nitsokhn Lid" ("Victory Song"), one of the "lost songs" marking the end of World War II and the defeat of the Nazis.

"Di Sapozkelekh" ("My Boots") a somber exposition by clarinet. A tune punctuated by halting rhythm.

A special note: "And the Angels Sing," from the Glenn Miller Band, started off as a klezmer tune.

Since the early 1900s there have been many iconic ensembles from all compass points (Israel, Argentina, Poland, Russia, the US, the UK), which became even more diverse with the diasporic nature of where families lived and moved. According to Professor David G. Hebert, "Traditional Jewish music is actually quite diverse and spread across multiple continents, from the *Shashmaqom* tradition of Bukhara (Mizrahi Jews) to the *Chaabi* of North Africa (Maghrebi Jews) and even genres

20

among the Beta Israel of Ethiopia, or young genres in the Americas, such as what developed from the predominantly Jewish composers of Tin Pan Alley." Once an individual or family moves to a new location, he says, there are other influences upon the culture: "Connections between musical sound and a sense of place are quite complex, since migrating people bring traditional sounds with them to new places, where they are impacted both by the materials available (for instruments) and the musical traditions that surround them in the new location."

Anna Shternshis, a cultural historian specializing in Soviet Jewish culture, talks about "lost" Yiddish songs of World War II that she came across while conducting research in Ukraine. These songs were from the Nazi-run ghettos located in Transnistria, a huge body of decades-unseen, unheard and uncatalogued work. "I would not say it's klezmer music. Most of it borrows from Ukranian, Romanian and Soviet music. There are some influences of Yiddish theater songs such as 'My Shtetele Beltz' and 'Kinder Yorn'." Shternshis first heard Yiddish songs from her family, then on stage in Moscow, and later, got to know Michael Alpert in 1997 when he came to Oxford Summer program to run a program about klezmer music.

PIONEERS, CURRENT PLAYERS and EVENTS

The "First Wave" and "Second Wave" bands and musicians include Belf's Romanian Orchestra (c. 1908), Abe Schwartz (1881-1963), Dave Tarras (1895-1989),

Naftule Brandwein (1884-1936), Harry Kandel (1885-1943); followed by Klezmorim, The Klezmatics, the Klezmer Conservatory, Martin Schwartz and Brave Old World, Paul Pincus, Ben Holmes, and Hersh Gross and His Boiberiker Kapelye, among others. Today's bands expand on the theme in using humor and wit in their names as a reflection of the inventiveness of their music, and include Flying Bulgar Klezmer Band, Golem, Yale Strom & Hot Pstromi, Mames Babegenush, Klezmofobia, ChickenFat Klezmer Orchestra, Metro Klezmer Connection, Folk and Honey, Klezmer Kaos, The Klezmer King and the Kat Klezmer Trio.

EVENTS

The pandemic didn't put the kibosh on klezmer. Many streaming events were held and even better-attended than in the past. Festival organizers and venues have geared up to hold these music-filled experiences once again, this time live. A partial list includes:

Ashkenaz Festival (Toronto, Canada)
Festival Internacional de Música Sefardí (Cordoba, Spain)
Humboldt Jewish Music Jewish Music and Culture Festival (California, US)
Jewish Culture Festival
Jewish Culture Festival (Krakow, Poland)
Jewish Music Institute (London, UK)
Klezfest London
KlezKamp (New York, US)

KlezKanada
Klezmer Fest (Arizona, US)
Klezmer Querque (New Mexico, US)
KlezNorth (UK)
Kyiv Klezmer Fest (Ukraine)
Safed Klezmer Festival (Israel)
Yiddish New York
Yiddish Summer Weimar (Germany)
Yidstock (Massachusetts, US)

Klezmer for the Joyful Soul

PART II – The Interviews

PHIL ALEXANDER

Phil Alexander hails from Scotland and holds a first degree in Music, a Masters in Ethnomusicology, and completed his PhD in 2016, which examined how klezmer and Yiddish music have been reinterpreted and recreated in today's Berlin. He plays the accordion.

How did you get into klezmer?

It was when I was in college in Sheffield at about age 20 and the guy I was living with was a trombonist. He was in a street band playing gypsy tunes, klezmer, English folk tunes and Eastern European music. It piqued my curiosity and I was very instantly hooked. It brought together musically a lot of things that I loved, and I'm Jewish so there was also that to grab onto. After college I went back to London and worked as a musician with clarinetist Gregory Schechter, from whom I learnt a great deal. We played weddings and bar mitzvahs for about four years. It was a lot of fun.

My partner and I moved up to Edinburgh from London in 2002 and I had no intention of playing klezmer music. I expected to learn Scottish folk music. There's a great jazz scene in Glasgow and Edinburgh, and I was also tapping into that.

Founding our band Moishe's Bagel was accidental. A Chilean singer that I had met, Valentina Montoya-Martinez, was starting a tango band and asked if I played tango before. Also in the band was a fiddle player named Greg Lawson and accordionist Pete Garnett. I knew a great bass player, Mario Caribé, so he came into the band. We gelled as a musical unit and had an interest in the Eastern European sound so we found ourselves playing that, alongside the tangos. Then I thought, "Well, this is daft, let's get together and make it more official." Mario and I knew a terrific tabla and darabuka [Middle Eastern drum] player, Guy Nicolson, so we said "let's get him." We didn't have a name or any gigs yet. We sat down cross-legged, lit endless cigarettes and played music, and very quickly we had this brilliant sound. We knew we were onto something good.

Where do you draw the line between Yiddish music and klezmer?

Historically there's a separation between them. Klezmer was instrumental, for weddings and community ritual celebrations, and historically it's been all male; men playing in a dynastic caste system with a repertoire that was passed down. Yiddish songs were often sung by women and would have covered home, social life, love and politics and so on – the stuff of folk song more generally. That was until the mid-20th century. But the klezmer revival threw up a lot of amazing musicians like Michael Alpert, Adrienne Cooper and Lorin Sklamberg who are also excellent interpreters of klezmer songs. As a result, the lines have blurred much more, and now people often see themselves as part of a sort of klezmer-Yiddish musical complex. Many people in Yiddish singing are also connected to the klezmer world, and vice versa.

Historians and contemporary musicians will acknowledge the differences but also consider the overlap. A lot of those connected with the revival movement (some don't use that term) are often quite politicized with a new Yiddish consciousness, so Yiddish comes to occupy an important activist role.

For your British Academy ECR Fellowship that runs from Autumn 2019 through the summer of 2022, what does your research entail?

The Fellowship is developing all the time. From 2017-2019 I worked as postdoctoral Research Associate on the *Jewish Lives, Scottish Spaces* project (Universities of Glasgow and Edinburgh), looking at the cultural world of Jewish immigrants to Scotland in the late 19th and early 20th centuries. My British Academy ECR Fellowship (autumn 2019 - summer 2022) will allow me to take this work further, concentrating particularly on musical practice among Jews in early 20th century Scotland.

There was a wave of immigration from 1880 to 1925 to Scotland, principally to Glasgow and also Edinburgh. Looking at the music there, I discovered several interesting characters - immigrant Jews - who had written some great music, some of it "Jewish," some less so. The Fellowship is a chance to tell their stories. Some of these are people who died in the 1950s, so I spoke with their grandkids.

I'm hoping to also explore archives in Warsaw and Jerusalem, and looking creatively to reinterpret some of the music I find by getting friends in and producing new material. The initial output was going to be a book, but now it will likely be a number of articles and some creative projects with recordings and sound installations.

Although not that much is documented, what is documented includes information on cantor Isaac Hirshow, who was born in Velizh in Northwestern Russia. He worked in Warsaw, married, then moved to Glasgow in the early1920s where he worked as cantor for Garnethill synagogue for the next 30 years. He was the first person to get a degree in music from Glasgow University. He would have been in his 50s at that point. Not much has survived but there is a substantial cantata based on several prayers, a fine piece of work that has not yet been performed. One of my projects will be to realize a performance of this cantata for chamber orchestra and chorus.

Debbie Burke

What are some of your favorite songs?

We like to play a lot of traditional klezmer music: "Devotedly Buoyant" (that's what we know it as) which I learned from Gregori Schechter. We love it. We also like a slow hora from the [Wolff] Kostakowsky collection, a 3/8 processional that has some very magical moments; and standards like "A Night in the Garden of Eden" and "Odessa Bulgar." But the majority of our material is original composition, which brings together all our various influences. The strength of the band is the different musical positions we've come from; we can't help but apply that. Diversity is one of our strengths and we are pretty adept musicians. The music is very listenable and a challenge for audiences as they don't know where it's going to go next.

Why do you think as an artform that it has survived?

It's survived for lots of different reasons, some wrapped up in identity, some connected to music. The revival happened at the point when identity politics more generally was developing a significant cultural push, and in the early 70s you can see how a rediscovery of Jewish folk music – largely driven by second-generation Jewish Americans looking for meaningful roots – would fit into that. Over the last forty or more years, that has grown into a strong international movement. There's also a vibrant and vital education network for this music at places like Yiddish Summer Weimar. That helps a lot.

31

Aside from that, klezmer is a really exciting music to play. If you are a classically trained musician then you can put your technique to good use, and yet it's definitely not the same as playing a Mozart quartet. At the same time, lots of klezmer is dance music and so there is something very grounded about it. The way jazz looks for spaces between notes, those are integral to klezmer music. It has a thrill and a virtuosic energy but also a very sociable, communal aesthetic that you find in a lot of folk music.

Where will it go? That will depend on some really good, new composers. Think about jazz, and the way the language changed with bebop and hard bop. Wayne Shorter was writing new standards, not Tin Pan Alley or the Great American Songbook. In klezmer, we're in many ways still at the Great American Songbook stage.

The basis of education and dissemination is pretty well formed. Can it develop in a way that takes that tradition and pushes it outward somewhere? We might still be waiting for a new breakthrough. There are a number of truly world-class artists, but right now I would also say that the klezmer envelope could still be pushed a little more. There are little moments but a revolution hasn't happened yet.

What's your book about?

My book *Sounding Jewish in Berlin* explores the Berlin klezmer scene of the past few decades. My main question is what happens to traditional music when it comes face to face with the modern cosmopolitan city;

how does it stay audible? It's a good story that takes in Berlin Street and bar culture, amazing musicians, complicated German-Jewish history, and some very cool music! In particular, I'm showing that since about 2010 a new grassroots scene has grown up which is far more internationally connected. This new wave builds on a space made for klezmer by earlier musicians (most of whom are also still very active), but it also takes it forward in some very dynamic ways. It's a symbiotic relationship – the city affects the music but the music also shapes the city.

ROBERT BECK

Robert Beck, clarinetist, plays in the band Fire, Rain and Espresso. He's based in Papenburg, Germany.

When did you first pick up the clarinet? Which range (size) clarinet do you mostly perform with?

I started clarinet when I was ten years old. Originally, I wanted to play saxophone, but my teacher insisted I should start with clarinet. I stuck with it, although now I sometimes also play the saxophone. And I also like playing the bass clarinet in my trio, adding another colour.

What was your first introduction to klezmer?

My dad took me to a concert of the band "Colalaila," with the clarinet player Irith Gabriely. I loved the music and the vibes and started to play some tunes myself. Mostly together with my dad, earning some pocket money as a street musician.

What captivated you about it?

The energy, the contrasts and immediacy, with which the players were approaching their instruments. I love to listen to klezmer-related music with is open to other genres, like the music of David Krakauer, John Zorn or Ben Caplan.

What inspires you when you are composing for a klezmer piece?

I don't intentionally compose klezmer pieces, although of course the sound and feeling off this music always are present in my ears. An inspiration can be for example a certain image or mood or even sort of "story" I want to catch. But it also can be a certain harmonic shape other than just a phrase sounding good on my instrument I then try to transform to a whole piece.

What was your favorite collaboration?

At the moment, I enjoy playing the most playing with my colleagues from "Firasso," Nils Imhorst on bass and Marko Kassl on accordion. This band is great fun and for myself a perfect laboratory to try out new music. I also enjoy working with actors and dancers very much.

What other genres do you play that you feel are related to or take some element of klezmer?

I love jazz, which I have been listening to since I was a kid, I also played saxophone in a funk-band when I was a student. Unfortunately, my improvisation skills are not very good, but I am working on it. And I also have a great love for Balkan music. I love the feeling and the odd rhythms.

"*As classically trained musicians we are like chameleons, playing whatever piece of music is put on our music stand. In our job as orchestral musicians, we are used to performing a Mahler symphony, a Gershwin concert, Bach's St. John Passion, a Wagner opera or pop concerts with acts like Orchestral Manoeuvres in the Dark or Elvis Costello in quick succession, adapting to any style, in order to serve the music to the best of our abilities. Yes, one could say that we, Klezmer-ish, are not born into the culture of klezmer music, but at the end of the day all music boils down to the expression of human emotions. Love, hate, joy, sorrow...no culture can claim ownership over these fundamentally human feelings. We all have the ability to experience them. Klezmer is a musical style that reflects so many aspects of human life, and so it seemed natural for us to want to throw ourselves into this fascinating tradition. We feel privileged to be the vessel through which some of these amazing tunes come to life. We become messengers of great ideas; we don't own them.*"

- Marcel Becker, bass player, Klezmer-ish; leader of the double bass section of the Royal Liverpool Philharmonic Orchestra

GLENN DICKSON

Glenn Dickson is a clarinetist, composer and bandleader of Shirim and Naftule's Dream. He plays solo on the new release "Dreams and Meditations" and "Strange News."

How did you learn about klezmer?

I went to New England Conservatory in Boston at the time that the Klezmer Conservatory Band (KCB) formed. I didn't really hear them initially, but my girlfriend at the time gave me an early Giora Feidman klezmer recording and that was probably my first exposure. I loved the vocal quality of the clarinet and the energy of the music so I started transposing the tunes and working out the inflections and ornaments.

Then at some point I heard the KCB and my classmate, Don Byron, playing the stuff and they had their first recording. I got hooked and spent many hours

---

figuring the stuff out. It was very different from the classical sound I was working on at school. I played a set of tunes I learned on my senior recital at the Conservatory, and that set things in motion towards a certain trajectory for me.

When the KCB accordionist, Barry Shapiro, left that band, he wanted to start a new band. He knew that I had been working on the music so he asked me to join him. At that point he gave me all the repertoire tapes, recordings of the players from the 1920-1950s that he had from the KCB, and I also searched source recordings. This led to a deeper study of the style, learning from the old generations rather than the current generation.

When did you start playing clarinet? When did you first start playing klezmer?

I started playing clarinet in elementary school, around 1969. I started learning klezmer in my third year of college, around 1980.

How did you reinterpret "The Nutcracker" for klezmer and how did you get the feel of Eastern European music across in the production?

Our klezmer version of "The Nutcracker Suite" came about because in the mid-1990s the band was self-producing concerts every Christmas day at the Coolidge Corner Theatre in the heart of a large Jewish neighborhood just outside of Boston. They were very popular shows. Often, we would sell out two shows at the theater. We were thinking of novel things to do for the concerts and came up with the idea of a klezmer version of "The Nutcracker Suite." It wasn't a huge musical stretch, as much of the music has a lot of Russian folk influence like klezmer, so our trombonist David Harris and accordionist Michael McLaughlin took the tunes and changed some rhythms here, some notes there and we played them with klezmer inflections and feel and it worked great. It was very popular so we recorded it. The thing is, although it seems like it would be a real shticky novelty, I actually think it has a lot of integrity and works really well. And culturally it really resonated with a lot of people. Jewish people get inundated with Christmas that time of the year and it twisted the music into a Jewish/Hanukah setting.

We later worked with Ellen Kushner, author and National Public Radio host, to create a radio play which she wrote and we used the Nutcracker music, expanded with more tunes from the ballet, and it was called "The Golden Dreydl, a Klezmer Nutcracker for Hanukah." Rykodisc released it and it was made into a theater production in New York.

Talk about klezmer fusion. What specific elements do you keep and which do you modify in order to create fusion?

Well, we had been playing a lot of concerts and I was feeling that the music, being dance music, was not always suited for extended concerts, one dance tune after another. I started writing things which had more development and threw in some improvised sections, making it something an audience could engage in as a listening spirit.

My first pieces stuck to traditional sounds but as I wrote, naturally other elements crept in. I just did what came naturally and what was interesting to me. At a certain point some of the older members of the audience, who knew this music from Europe, got upset with what we were doing. I remember one concert when an older gentleman came right up to the stage and yelled, between tunes, "This is not our music!" At that point I realized I had to split the product up so that we could keep exploring in our new group Naftule's Dream and keep playing traditional music with Shirim. Shirim had already released the "Naftule's Dream" album, and you can hear the divide. Some of the tunes are completely traditional renditions of klezmer music and Yiddish songs; other tunes are definitely pushing the envelope, bringing in jazz and rock elements. So, it was a very organic process, not a decision to create a "fusion."

After that we were able to keep having fun playing traditional music in Shirim (and family fun pieces like the "Nutcracker" and "Pincus & the Pig" with Maurice Sendak) and let ourselves go in Naftule's Dream, which brought in elements of free jazz, edgy rock, anything we felt like.

Usually there was some connection to klezmer and Yiddish music, either the rhythmic foundation or the tonal foundation. Sometimes it is not obvious, other times it is. I also got into setting Yiddish poems from some pretty wild poets to music that wasn't really Jewish-derived at all. We were just having fun. But it succeeded beyond our wildest dreams. John Zorn released three of our albums on his Tzadik label, and we started touring Europe starting with a great concert at the Berlin Jazz Festival.

How did Shirim start up and how did you decide on your band mates?

When Barry Shapiro left the KCB, he knew I was playing klezmer on my own and asked me. My girlfriend at the time was a singer and very interested in Yiddish; and beyond that, we just sought out good musicians who were willing to learn the music. At that point, 1982, it was all about searching out old 78rpm records, transferring them to cassette and spending a lot of time transcribing and learning the tunes. Very little written music was available except some old Yiddish theater songbooks and Yiddish folksong books, but they weren't that valuable compared to learning the soul of the music from the old recordings.

Are there classic klezmer songs you enjoy playing?

Really, I cycle through tunes, always learning new ones which become my favorites for a while and then I move on to others. Right now, I am spending a lot of time with the German Goldenshteyn transcriptions (a lot of great tunes) and the Beregovski transcriptions.

What are some of your own klezmer compositions? Describe one or two of them.

"The Black Wedding" is one of my most-recorded pieces, I mean by other bands as well as my own. To be honest, I wanted to write something simple. It just has two chords and is in the Freygish mode and is based on the "bulgar" or "freylakh" rhythm groove. But after the first two melodic sections it got away from me and I found a way to make the freygish scale very disjunct and sort of scary sounding, and then I took it into a rock variation of the melody (in unison with the band), and into a groove vamp for improvising. It ends up with another unison variation on the melody, then the straight melody played in unison with the clarinet improvising on top. It is a fun tune to play, is not that complex, but makes a good impression. It has been recorded by rock bands and klezmer bands in the US and Europe.

"Waiting" was used by Woody Allen in his film "Deconstructing Harry" as the theme for the main character's wife. On that one I used a more Middle Eastern groove to create a three-section melody in the Freygish mode (mostly) and the third section is the contrasting "waiting" section. I think it is just a nice melody which goes someplace. We improvise in a jazzy Middle Eastern "Taksim" style.

Why do you feel the clarinet allows you to express yourself more than another instrument?

The clarinet is great because of the wide range, from the very mellow, warm and woody low notes to the very pleasant middle range and then the high range which can soar over a band. It has a wider range than the other winds like sax or flute, or any of the brass. It also allows for very voice-like inflections like note bends, growls and great articulation possibilities. The flexible pitch is really special, allowing for portamentos, like a string, and laughing and crying sounds.

Other comments?

One thing I am very grateful for is the work we got to do with Maurice Sendak's "Pincus & the Pig, a Klezmer Tale." After the klezmer "Nutcracker" we got the idea to do a klezmer version of Prokofiev's "Peter and the Wolf." We were looking around for someone to rewrite the story and approached different well-known children's authors and it just so happened we contacted Maurice Sendak at the right time. He was working on "Brundibar" with Tony Kushner and was depressed from being steeped in the Holocaust theme and this gave him a little break from the heaviness. He renamed Peter after his father, Pincus, and his relatives in Poland had referred to anti-Semites as pigs, so it all worked for him in a very personal way. He liked a story where the Jewish boy comes out on top.

Again, the Russian music was easy to translate into klezmer music, and Maurice drew on the Yiddish he heard in his house as a boy to transform the story beautifully (it must be noted that we have since learned that Arthur Yorinks helped with the story). He also made perfect illustrations of each character for the CD cover and booklet. We went to his house in Connecticut and recorded him performing the narration and I think it came out great. He sounds like a Jewish grandfather telling a story. That is a gem of an album that is still not well-known enough. John Zorn released it on Tzadik.

I am sure I could talk about this for hours, but these are important points: I feel like Shirim and "Naftule's Dream" were/are important bands in the genre, with a big creative contribution to an often staid culture. The traditional tunes we wrote, the arrangements of the classical pieces, the concept of "Naftule's Dream" were radical and ground-breaking at the time, and I think all of the music holds up and is still fresh. We were one of the first bands John Zorn chose for his Radical Jewish Culture series. It set off a whole movement.

ORAN ETKIN

A New York-based jazz clarinet player and composer, Oran Etkin's recent music includes "Un Tour du Monde Avec Clara Net ("Timbalooloo")" and "Finding Friends Far from Home."

How did you discover klezmer?

Growing up I had more Israeli music around me than klezmer. I was born in Israel and moved to Boston when I was four.

I got into klezmer when I was in high school out of curiosity. Growing up in Boston there was the Klezmer Conservatory Band. There were a lot of creative things happening like The Klezmatics and John Zorn and that whole scene. I got into that as another flavor I could add into my music. I was getting into a lot of different music from around the world in high school and college. When I did my master's at Manhattan School of Music, I had the opportunity to study with David Krakauer. He showed me how to really dive into klezmer and get the sound and appreciate the nuances of it and how it comes from cantorial singing. As a clarinet player you can make it sound like a cantor.

I started with piano when I was four or five and then violin when I was eight, saxophone when I was nine, guitar at 10. That guitar teacher also taught me composition and improvisation. I started studying at age 14 with George Garzone, the great saxophonist from Boston. When I went to high school, that's when I got into clarinet, because I'd heard the Mozart Clarinet Concerto. I was going to summer camps in Israel that were classical-based. At first when I got the clarinet from school, I wanted to participate in more chamber music and got deeper into it. I decided to do my undergrad in classical clarinet and composition at Brandeis University. I did a double major with economics.

I studied with Tom Martin of the Boston Symphony Orchestra on clarinet and kept going to George Garzone. Charlie Banacos was a legendary teacher with a three-year waiting list who taught Michael Brecker, all these guys, and he had half-hour slots back to back to back, ear training, exercise, play a tune, tell a joke, you're out of there. Then I came to New York and I decided to do my master's at the Manhattan School of Music and split my lessons between sax (Dick Oatts, Joe Temperley, Dave Liebman) and clarinet with Dave Krakauer.

I had a band that played some klezmer and that was exploring it and getting into the improvisational side of klezmer. It was at this time we were inspired by different ways of taking klezmer into jazz and rock.

Your first public performance?

It was probably a Jewish wedding. That was before I studied with Dave Krakauer. When I moved to New York I got called for some Jewish weddings and I worked with Joey Weisenberg, who was a student at Columbia and was leading the band. He was into traditional klezmer. He was more of a purist – like, no improvisation – and I thought it was really great to work with people who were deeper into it like Joe.

It's a social music. It's amazing how you have these weddings and the people attending don't normally listen to klezmer but once it starts playing, they react in a way that feels like home to them.

You've toured, then put together an album based on your experiences. Why?

It started with 2014's "Gathering Light." Instead of writing the music and then touring it, I wanted the touring to be part of the creative process. So first we toured Indonesia, China, Israel and West Africa and then I wrote music inspired by these melodies and rhythms that I encountered in my travels. Now I'm extending this idea with Open Arms Project, which is a series of singles that I recorded around the world collaborating with traditional masters in Zimbabwe, Brazil, Czech Republic and other places.

In this world there are experts at bringing the darkness, fear and hatred out of people (like some politicians), but as musicians, we bring out the light. Wherever we go we connect through music. That was the concept of "Gathering Light."

Where else has klezmer brought you, musically?

A collaboration that touches on the klezmer side is with the Roma musicians in Czech Republic. I've been working with a festival called the Mladi Ladi Jazz Festival and I've been playing there every year since 2014. They have a big project where they include the Roma population which is very underserved. It's with Roma, Czech and Slovak musicians and mixes in Roma music, some klezmer music and an open, improvisational jazz approach. That was really amazing. The connections between Roma music and klezmer, and between the Jewish history and the Roma history, are so similar and so symbiotic. I felt like my klezmer background got a new place to grow.

Last April's Mladi Ladi Jazz Festival was rescheduled several times, but hopefully it will be held this coming September.

What's happening in the klezmer scene in New York?

Things are starting to open up in the music scene as a whole. I'm curating an outdoor concert series in

Bellport Long Island. It's the Full Moon Concert Series at Mama Farm in Bellport.

A prognosis for klezmer?

I think it's great to see it as an evolving music. I think a lot of times there are people who try to capture it as "authentic music." With any art form (traditional art forms included), you can never really get to the authentic source of it, because the great klezmer musicians in America were very influenced by American music as well. And in Europe they were also influenced by regional music. I think it's important to understand the depth of the source of the music, understanding it from the inside and not putting it as a color on top of things, which is what I had been doing before I started working with David Krakauer, like "oh let me sprinkle this on" without knowing the depth of what it was.

Once you get deep into it and love it, it becomes part of who you are. Once I got deep into these old recordings and tried to get these sounds on the clarinet, these things called *krekhts,* how you get the real vocal break of the Jewish vocal sound, it would come out in all kinds of other settings. I'd be playing with African musicians and putting in these krekhts and playing with this flavor. It was never like let me just put it in here, it was not conscious, it was just because I was deep into that music and I loved it, that I was starting to phrase it that way.

I'm sure there were elements of Louis Armstrong in how I phrased klezmer. It was what I grew up with.

From the age of nine to 14 all I would listen to was Louis Armstrong and New Orleans music. I'm sure that influences how I play klezmer. And some African drumming comes out when I play jazz. All this stuff adds up.

The trick is loving the deep, original stuff, the roots of the music, and not "just let me throw things in." Once you get into it you realize this is really soulful music.

SUSI EVANS

Susi Evans plays clarinet, accordion, whistles and bagpipe. Her new book is *"Shades of Folk/Klezmer Playbook"* and it contains 50 traditional klezmer tunes.

When did you first hear klezmer?

I first heard it in Hungary in 2000 in a classical clarinet course. I was about to go to the Royal Academy of Music in London and I was just studying to be a classical clarinet player. One of clarinet professors there (in Hungary) started to play klezmer music and I thought that's a cool thing, I never heard the clarinet play anything apart from classical music.

The following year at the Academy there was a flyer for KlezFest in London and it was actually the first

KlezFest. I asked if I could come along, and that was the beginning. I was at the right place at the right time. The energy and the fun and the vibe of the music at KlezFest were great. We were all just playing on the lawn outside and people were able to play without needing sheet music.

I don't know how they knew what to play. I was a good clarinetist but I didn't know what to do to jump in. I'd never learned anything by ear. I went back and tried to learn them all by ear. I was 20. Now, I've been a faculty member of KlezFest for the last five years.

My mom is a bit of a musician. She plays bagpipes and has a lot of musical friends. She plays klezmer and sees it as a folk music rather than a music of her heritage, and she told me to go for it.

I founded a klezmer band after that with six or seven people in my class and we used to meet at the RAM. We had a hippie-type accordion player and people would say, "Oh yeah, that's Susi's band." I was asked to do a concert in the huge Dukes Hall, a proper concert hall. The Academy is in London and they have a lot of Jewish supporters who love to come for the concerts. It was advertised on the program on the night it was taking place and it completely sold out.

Why did all these people come to see this disheveled-looking band? We had learned 15 tunes all by heart and we collected a few musicians along the way.

How did you get into clarinet?

In school, I played recorder and violin too, and I learned to read music.

I wanted to play the flute and went to the music shop and asked the manager for the flute and he said, "Here's a flute, but you don't really have the right shaped mouth. Why don't you try the clarinet?" I took it home and I would sit and play it. I got far quite quickly at age 10!

What did you learn about klezmer in your formal training while at the Royal Academy, Purcell or Plovdiv?

No klezmer training at the RAM. At Plovdiv Academy of Music and Dance, it was a summer school organized by Larry Weiner, also well-known in the klezmer scene.

I've been to the Plovdiv seminar six times. Bulgarian music is more challenging than klezmer and tends to go at a fast pace. One of the biggest differences is that it's a living tradition that has continued developing, whereas klezmer had a big shift in its development from being an Eastern European music that suddenly became an American music.

How did you get involved in Yiddish Summer Weimar?

Yiddish Summer Weimar has good links with Klezfest London. Last year, during lockdown, YSW put on a summer program where everything was taught outdoors. It was a lot to organize, but they're planning it again this year.

Do you feel a tie to your ancestry when you perform or compose?

No, because my heritage is not Jewish. In fact, my family has Viking ancestry.

What was the scene immediately before COVID, and do you feel there is a strong interest in klezmer in the UK today?

Yes, there's a scene. There are a few professional bands here in London that play just klezmer and do weddings, and a few other bands like She'Koyokh who combine klezmer with Balkan music and play some festivals and concerts. Then there's the amateur scene, the people who go to KlezFest and attend jam sessions.

During the lockdown the jam sessions continued on Zoom, or they'd just go to the park and have a session.

What are some of your favorite traditional songs?

I did an album with Szilvia Csaranko [accordion/ piano] on the Dave Tarras repertoire, who was so versatile as a musician.

There is so much you can choose from with Dave Tarras' repertoire: Moldavian, Greek, Polish, the American style with a bit of Yiddish swing. What I like is the variety. In a concert we'll play the sad ones. I love playing low and soft on clarinet. I like to play in the bottom octave. I play fiery and strong when I need to lead the band.

I'm learning trumpet and I'll play klezmer on it. Doing the fills and connecting lines sound good on trumpet.

How long did it take to write the "Klezmer Playbook" with Szilvia and what was that process like?

This was our lockdown project last year. We wanted to do a book that had popular tunes that we know people enjoy playing. So the idea is a book of 50 tunes that are all popular, and you can learn these and then join in the jam session. We recorded play-alongs for the tunes and sold quite a few of them.

We invited everybody we know who had a copy of the book to be in a club. That way, in the online workshops and jam sessions, we didn't have to send out sheet music. In the workshops we work on two tunes from the book in detail. We were amazed how popular these sessions were – there were 80 people in our first Zoom meeting and 100 people in the next one. We teach the workshop bilingually (in English and German). We record the sessions and are still running them.

RICHARD FAY

Richard Fay is a Senior Lecturer in Education, Manchester Institute of Education, The School of Environment, Education and Development (SEED), Manchester UK

Talk about your journey into klezmer and where that's taken you.

In 1982, I bought *"Klezmer Music 1910-1942,"* the first record in my klezmer library of loo+ records/CDs. It caught my eye as I flicked through the racks at the local music store. No idea why, but so began my obsession with this musical "Other" (I have no Jewish affiliation). It's a passion that has lasted forty years, withstood the disappointments of fruitless searches for klezmer remnants in Poland in the 1980s, and has blossomed into a network of projects, friendships, recordings, and teaching here in Manchester.

An intercultural educator by day, by night and instinct, I'm a composer and intercultural musician with klezmer center stage. Back in 2011, I co-founded the Michael Kahan Kapelye (The University of Manchester klezmer ensemble). It performs locally (e.g., Chanukah concerts at the Manchester Jewish Museum and events for the Muslim-Jewish Forum, the Association of Jewish Refugees and a local Jewish residential home). These days, I teach the ensemble with Daniel J. Mawson, a former student from the ensemble's early years. Together, we also write about our klezmer work (including a forthcoming article in the *Language and Intercultural Communication* journal), and give talks to community organizations such as Limmud.

Manchester-raised and of part Irish heritage, I devised *Amid the Mirk Over the Irk: When Irish Meets Klezmer* in 2015. This show combines the twin pillars of my musical life. It builds on an imaginary meeting in the 1880s of musicians from the immigrant slums on either side of Manchester's River Irk: on one side the Jewish community in Red Bank, and on the other the Irish community in Angel Meadow. The show involves klezmer and Irish trad musicians exploring commonalities and differences between these two musical cultures. We perform it every few years alongside other klezmer-oriented shows (including *Vessels of Song: Journeys into the Worlds of Klezmer*).

After all these years, the klezmer soundscape has lost none of its power over me. It retains its grip on my musical imaginings in ways beyond expectation when that first record sleeve caught my eye.

"Upon hearing klezmer for the first time, I was immediately drawn to the dance vibe, the beat, the pulse. At the time I first heard klezmer, about 25 years ago, I was well established as a classical flutist, with a career immersed in teaching at the college level and a fine symphony position. I had my two children and husband. Did I need to now learn a totally different kind of music? Yes! I heard the modes, the scales, the sorrowful wailing alongside the excitement and it grabbed me hard. I wanted to learn to play this stuff in the most authentic way and was told to go to KlezKamp in the Catskills (NY). I went, I learned what I could without a flute specialty and listened to the old recordings. I love improvising in much the same way that musicians did in the Baroque period. I enjoy playing fast, exuberant, more technically demanding tunes that also benefit from the afterglow of the impressive factor, to be cheaply honest. Equally, I literally melt into ornamenting the slow tunes, allowing each, plus the flute - and myself - to get totally lost in the soulful vibe. For me the flute is my voice. I love the contribution we can make to the whole: the sparkle and the soul that is added to the overall mix. The music itself bit me hard and became a true wow for my heart."

- Adrianne Greenbaum, klezmer flutist and professor at Mount Holyoke College

IRITH GABRIELY

Irith Gabriely plays klezmer clarinet but is no stranger to Mozart. Her recent albums include "The City Never Sleeps" and "Five Angels."

How did you first learn about klezmer?

Growing up in Israel, I actually grew up with klezmer music, especially because part of my family was Orthodox. We were often invited to their Chasidic weddings where they hired klezmer bands to play. On every family gathering and every holiday we use to sing the Jewish and Hebrew songs that I later played, improvised and accompanied.

Our Jewish way of life goes back to Poland before the Second World War. My parents and grandparents immigrated to Palestine before the war. Not only were their lives saved, but they brought this whole rich and wonderful tradition with them.

As soon as I put my hands on an instrument, I could immediately play whatever I hear. My parents and grandparents used to literally beg me to play one song after another along with their singing. They also loved to listen with tears in their eyes.

How did you first get the name "Queen of Klezmer" – is that a huge responsibility?

After the awards that I got at the international Festival in Tzfat, later at the Edinburgh Festival and then after a big concert in Munich, a journalist wrote about me and my show in a magazine: "She is the queen of klezmer." I liked it and started using it as a title in my resumés. And yes, it is a responsibility and a big honor that has been based on my solid classical upbringing, the many years of being the principal clarinetist at the opera and state orchestra of Darmstadt, Germany, followed by concerts as a soloist and conductor in front of several orchestras. I take most of the styles and genres of music including traditional klezmer and deliver my knowledge, namely the combination of music and the Jewish tradition.

This has not only built bridges between the different genres, but also between different cultures. I have several intercultural and interreligious projects going on; among them, an exchange with an Arabic youth orchestra from Haifa, Israel.

What is the most important thing you've learned from playing?

That people love it. For some reason the audience can't get enough klezmer. Maybe because this music is very emotional. It expresses a wide range of emotions. This music is a very rich language of the soul that speaks to them.

It doesn't hurt to put more feelings even into Bach, Mozart or any other musical style.

What was required mentally to transition from playing classical music at Darmstadt to playing klezmer in smaller ensembles?

As I feel at home in both styles, there is no problem switching. It's like growing up speaking two mother languages.

My first klezmer band in Darmstadt was spontaneously created. This is the story: A friend of mine, a conductor in the opera, wanted to learn about Jewish life. So I said to him, "You know what? Tonight is Shavuot and there is a party in the JComm. Let's go there after the opera."

When we arrived, someone was playing the accordion and people were dancing. Spontaneously I took out my clarinet and joined the session. It turned out that the accordion player was Moritz Neumann, a prominent figure in the Jewish community in our area. That was the beginning of my first klezmer band in Germany in 1980. Soon after, the Hebrew teacher who played the violin and the cantor who sang joined us and the four of us started touring all over Germany.

Do you feel the clarinet allows you to authentically express yourself?

In my opinion any instrument well-played can be authentic and expressive. The violin, for example, has much more expression than the clarinet. Unfortunately, I did not learn the violin. I wish I had!

What are some of your favorite songs in klezmer?

Difficult to answer that one. If they're arranged and played well, I love all of them. I get excited about prayers, which are rhythmical, that could become a dance, like for example "Adon Olam," "Yedid Nefesh," "Ele Chamda Libi," "El Adon," etc.

STEVEN GREENMAN

Steven Greenman is a violinist/educator/composer who is as much at home as a soloist in a symphony orchestra as he is playing Eastern European folk music.

How did you learn about klezmer?

I heard a few recordings back in the late 1980s but had a serendipitous summer in 1989 that got me hooked. That summer I participated in a classical music festival in Graz, Austria, and played klezmer and Yiddish music on the streets with a local American-born musician, Joshua Horowitz, together with my classical colleagues from the festival. After this experience, I met several folks at home who were performing klezmer music including Walt Mahovlich and Bert Stratton.

Do you feel that klezmer reflects either a social, political, historical or spiritual sensibility?

All of the above. The Yiddish folk arts revival (or revitalization) that began back in the 1970s and continues to this day has always drawn its inspiration from the labor movements and progressive politics from the early 20th century. In addition, contemporary Yiddish/klezmer culture has always been about the serious study, preservation and expansion of the historical models of performance and practice. On the spiritual side, the folks involved have mainly included secular/non-religious Jews and non-Jews. To these folks, Yiddish culture gives them a sense of belonging to a special creative group with its own socially motivated spiritual agenda.

Why do you think as an art form that it has survived?

The deep interest of second and third generation American Jews in the 1970s sparked a full-scale study of old 78 rpm recordings and interactions with older generations of klezmer musicians. This led to the creation of KlezKamp and subsequent Yiddish folk arts and culture festivals that propagated the music and art in both traditional and contemporary ways. There are Yiddish folk arts festivals all over the world. Klezmer music has survived and flourished due to this by training eager young artists who have carried the tradition further. One needs to look no further than the continuous creation of new klezmer works, both traditional and those that fuse with other musical traditions. There is an excitement to the music that draws folks in as well as a soulful component that moves people.

Have you been aware of more interest in it recently?

Overall, I would say there is more interest among people around the world, although the product at times has been oversaturated. On the professional side, many musicians used to be able to make a decent living playing klezmer music for weddings and bar/bat mitzvahs, but this has diminished considerably in the Jewish community over the last 25 years from its peak in the mid-1990s. The Yiddish revival was always a relatively small group of highly ambitious people competing for limited performance and teaching venues. The greater Jewish communities have not fully embraced Yiddish culture even with its amazing contemporary sounds and creative expressions.

What instrument do you play and what are some of your favorite songs in klezmer?

I am a professional violinist and my favorite klezmer tunes are the artistic listening tunes such as the *dobridens* and the rubato free-rhythm pieces that evoke cantorial chanting. I have composed a substantial number of traditional klezmer pieces for dancing and for listening, and these are some of my most favorite to perform.

Talk about the sense of community, and what brings the audience to it?

The musicians involved in performing, composing and teaching klezmer music (and Yiddish dance) are a tight-knit community, with the desire to continue to preserve the traditional style and to go beyond that. The greater Yiddish community includes these artists as well as lovers of Yiddish culture in general. There are many folks internationally who are curious about the music who are then drawn in and captivated by the emotions of it.

In the field, I am a performer/educator/composer of the music and have performed with many ensembles internationally and lead master classes of the music at universities, schools, festivals and much more.

JIM GUTTMAN

Jim Guttman is a bassist and plays in the Klezmer Conservatory Band. He's also a leader for Jim Guttmann's Bessarabian Breakdown.

Was your initial attraction to klezmer because you grew up listening to it, or did a musical or spiritual exploration bring you there?

Short version: My musical exploration brought me there.

Long version: After college, I was playing in a rock band and driving a cab in New York City. I ended up moving to Boston for a master's program in Mass Communications and, playing bass guitar, joined with a singer/songwriter and his woodwind-playing brother who happened to have a string bass. I borrowed the bass and was hooked. Over the next several years I studied, practiced and, with no particular genre of music in mind, explored the worlds of jazz and classical music, blues and bluegrass.

While playing with the Boston version of Jaki Byard's *Apollo Stompers* comprised mostly of New England Conservatory students and a few loose electrons like me, I met Hankus Netsky, who had written an arrangement of Lee Morgan's "Oh What a Night" for the band. When we ran into each other in February of 2018, he asked if I'd be interested in playing some Jewish music, adding that the bass players at New England Conservatory weren't interested in playing music with such simple bass parts.

The student group that performed a few klezmer tunes and a couple of Yiddish songs at the end of a concert of Jewish music a few weeks later was received with excitement and enthusiasm, and was offered several gigs on the spot. That group of musicians ended up as the core of the Klezmer Conservatory Band.

How do you feel that the style reflects either a social, political, historical or spiritual sensibility?

Many of the klezmer musicians that I have met over the years, including Hankus Netsky and Andy Statman, have indicated that they were drawn to klezmer music through their grandparents' musical performances, record collections and/or active use of the Yiddish language. Audience members at KCB's early concerts talked about how the music took them back to earlier days in their lives at home when they heard Yiddish being spoken and klezmer music being played.

My own observations, shared by various colleagues, were that the klezmer revival paralleled the folk music revival of the '60s. The folk revival began as an exploration of traditional songs and styles that gradually merged with the protest movement and morphed into the popular songwriting era that replaced Tin Pan Alley and the Brill Building's "moon, June and spoon" pop song lyrics – songwriters like Bob Dylan, Gordon Lightfoot, James Taylor and Phil Ochs, among others.

The klezmer revival started in the same way with an exploration of the traditional styles. Gradually, the klezmer musicians of the revival began to blend klezmer with other musical forms and began to write their own new Yiddish songs.

What are the elements that resonate the most with you: the melodies, harmonies, rhythm, lyrics or other?

As a bass player I have been drawn to the underlying rhythms of music of multiple genres; klezmer, of course, but also jazz, blues, Afro-Cuban and American R&B.

Are there techniques specific to the genre you had to specifically learn?

Short version: A specific, aggressive attack with the bow to drive the music forward.

Long version: When I first encountered the music with what became the Klezmer Conservatory Band, many of the songs we were listening to and transcribing our parts from were early 20th century large, marching band-like ensembles with multiple trombones and a tuba holding down the rhythm. KCB started out as a large ensemble with instrumentation similar to those ensembles. The band had multiple trumpets, trombones, fiddles, clarinet and saxophone, piano and accordion and a full drum set replacing marching bass and snare drums. There was no tuba, just my string bass, often unamplified. Without really thinking about it, I had to develop an aggressive attack with the bow so that the bass's notes could cut through and provide the necessary harmonic and rhythmic support.

What are some of your favorite songs and why?

Abe Schwartz's "Philadelphia Sher" – In thinking about the answer to "why?" the Broadway musical's title "The Roar of the Greasepaint, the Smell of the Crowd" just popped into my head. Its positive, forward-moving energy, whether played by a quartet or a dodecahedron (well, just a 12-piece ensemble) seems to get people on their feet.

"Bessarabian Chusidl" – From the early years of KCB this song has captured my attention as a fusion candidate, both as a funky bass and drum duo and, eventually in my own band's arrangement as a large ensemble piece drawing on the sound of the legendary band Tower of Power with a rhythmic hint of the Caribbean.

Talk about the sense of community in klezmer.

As a bass player, almost all my musical activity is in ensembles. In klezmer music, as in other ethnic and popular dance music, I see the bass as part of a team, the engine that drives the music forward or the brakes that keep it from veering off course, helping to create the energy that keeps dancers moving and providing support for the virtuoso soloists when they strut their stuff.

"Klezmer is about energy. I think that certain music survives for centuries because it speaks to something that is intangible about the human experience. If you really want to express celebratory energy, klezmer is a really great tool to have in your toolbox."

- Glenn Hartman (accordion), The New Orleans Klezmer All Stars

CURTIS HASSELBRING

Curtis Hasselbring, aka "Curha," is a trombonist, guitarist and composer. One of his newest tracks is "Togar" on the album "Curha II."

You play several instruments. What are they? Would you say trombone is your primary instrument?

I started playing the trombone and guitar both around fifth grade. I also learned the piano during high school and college. Most of my formal training was spent learning the trombone and it is the instrument I play professionally the most (although I do a fair amount of guitar playing as well).

How were you introduced to klezmer?

Through playing with musicians in the downtown scene (associated with the Knitting Factory and the radical Jewish culture movement of the late 1980s-90s). I met Greg Wall in 1991 and Frank London in 1993 or 1994, and through them started doing various projects (more in the jazz vein). My first real traditional klezmer gig was playing for Ted Reichman's wedding with Frank's Klezmer Brass All Stars in 2001. Ted is an old friend whom I played with a lot at the time and I volunteered to play with Frank for his wedding which turned out to be an introduction into another world of music.

Why do you find the trombone most allows you to express yourself, particularly in this genre?

In klezmer, the trombone is more of a rhythm section instrument and generally plays less melody. I enjoy playing all sorts of roles as a trombonist and I see klezmer as another facet of what I like to do. I compare it to being a character actor.

Do you feel there is a crossover between klezmer and jazz and what does that sound like?

There has often been some sort of crossover between jazz players and klezmer musicians since it came to America in the 20th century. There is a high degree of instrumental virtuosity needed for both genres and players naturally incorporate whatever is current into their playing. When I moved to New York in the

'90s, there was a good deal of cross-genre experimentation with jazz, klezmer and Eastern European influences. The downtown music scene had people such as John Zorn, Marc Ribot, Frank London and Anthony Coleman combining things in interesting ways which is what drew me to that world.

Klezmer does not include improv per se and jazz is most definitely about that. What are your thoughts on this?

I think of a klezmer ensemble as being similar to a Dixieland group, where everybody knows the song and plays their roles, which I see as improvisation with specific parameters although some groups include longer solos (as opposed to the traditional "embellishments of the melody" approach).

What are some of the elements of the music that you really enjoy?

The melodic aspect. Also when it is played in the traditional way, there is a "swing" to the rhythmic feel that is pretty unique. The Klezmatics' drummer David Licht is a master of this.

What are some of the challenges in writing in this genre?

Most of my own compositions are not klezmer-based although there is definitely some subconscious inspiration. I have co-written some Golem songs that are coming out of the tradition. I try to be true to myself and not think in terms of fitting in with pre-existing klezmer tropes.

What were some of your most notable collabs in klezmer?

Working with Golem and Frank London would cover those highlights. Golem has always been a fun band, not super-traditional (by design) but high-energy. Some of my first playing with Frank's Klezmer Brass All Stars involved touring in Europe in a double bill with the Boban Marković Orchestra (one of the leading Serbian brass bands). That was quite exciting. They were a formidable group to share a bill with and we really had to play our best to keep up. We were outnumbered 2 to 1 and they had hits (they played the music from the soundtrack to Kusturica's "Underground") that got the crowds going. That being said, we held our own, energy-wise, and it was a fun hang. I also created a remix for Frank (under my electronica name "Curha") that ended up on one his Klezmer Brass All Star records ("Carnival Conspiracy") that I am proud of.

Talk about the different ensembles you are in and what is new for each of them as venues start to open up.

Right now, as far as klezmer goes, my only regular group is Golem. Last year was the band's 20th anniversary so I am hoping as things start up again, we will get to do something special for that.

What are some of your favorite klezmer classic tunes?

As weird as this seems, I don't know song titles (outside of the obvious mega-hits like "Hava Nagila" and "Tum Balalaika"). I like Frank's repertoire which includes some really great songs by now-deceased Romanian clarinetist German Goldenshtayn.

"I love clarinet in a klezmer band because it inspires joy. Nothing like klezmer brings an audience to their feet, dancing, singing, and joining the ah-ya-ya's. When our band plays the klezmer set, young and old delight together, what could be better than that?"

- David Kauffman, Sulam (band, Hebrew for *Ladder*), Vancouver, Canada.

DAVID KRAKAUER

A contemporary icon, David Krakauer is a masterful clarinetist and highly respected teacher with a wide influence on today's players.

How did you first get turned on to klezmer?

I was a fully formed professional musician in my early 30s when I first really got into klezmer music. I didn't grow up with it at all. To set the scene I want to mention how I got into jazz and off-the-page/non-classical music: As a kid I went to the High School of Music and Art in New York City, which was a kind of a paradise for me. It was an amazing place, a mix of kids from every neighborhood, every socioeconomic group and every race and ethnicity coming together to do music or visual arts. It was a crazy collection of creative types. We would hang out in front of the school shooting the breeze and exchanging ideas. We were all together in a hotbed of creativity and I met some amazing musicians and visual artists there.

Music and Art was located at 135th Street and Convent Avenue next to the City College campus. One morning (as was my habit before classes started) I was sitting in front of the school on St. Nicholas Terrace which was a street at the top of a big hill. My best friend, Anthony Coleman (an incredible jazz pianist, composer and now educator at the New England Conservatory Improv Department), was coming up the stairs from the subway and heard me playing Sidney Bechet licks on my soprano saxophone. That's how we met. He was into Jelly Roll Morton, Duke Ellington and Monk plus writing his own music and leading his own band. So he signed me up to play tenor and clarinet.

I told him I only played classical music on the clarinet, and that I didn't play jazz on it. He said *why not?* Jazz clarinet in 70s was not that hip so I really wanted be a tenor player. But that was kind of a pipe dream since the reality was that I didn't practice the sax at all. It never became my voice. In fact, the instrument I was spending hours a day practicing was clarinet. Starting to improvise on the clarinet during that time really brought my two worlds together and changed the course of my life.

A little related anecdote: One day Anthony and I went to a concert of one of Leon Russianoff's students (Russianoff was my teacher and was world-renowned for having taught many of the top symphonic players at the time). After the concert we went up to Leon to say hello. I introduced Anthony as a great

Ellington scholar. And Russianoff said (somewhat conspiratorially): "You know I taught Jimmy Hamilton... do you think I made his playing too clean?"

I was deeply into jazz and classical as a kid. But in my early 20s when I went to college, I got kind of freaked out and had a crisis of confidence. I felt that I'd never be original enough to really play jazz in the way that I wanted to. I was also turned off by a lot of the fusion stuff I was hearing; so that combined with the fear that I couldn't find my own original voice led me to abandon jazz. I was afraid I didn't have what it took. I quit and focused on classical music in early 20s went to the Paris Conservatory.

When I got out of college at Sarah Lawrence, I went to Juilliard for my masters   with Russianoff.   After finishing school, I was freelancing, playing orchestral, chamber and contemporary classical music. But after about 10 years of doing that, when I was in my early 30s, I felt like I had thrown the baby out with bathwater; I missed off-the-page music-making, improv, and creativity.

At the time I lived on 80thand Broadway across from the Jewish deli Zabar's. One day I heard an incredible sound wafting up to my window and it was klezmer. I had heard a few records here and there plus a few years earlier I heard the great Eastern European Jewish clarinet master Dave Tarras play live (in 1980). He was already quite elderly but he still had such a sound. He couldn't play technically so well anymore but the sound and energy that he had gave me goosebumps.

He had an authority and a vibe that reminded me of all great jazz players I worshipped.

When I heard the sound of that klezmer band wafting up to my window, something clicked in my brain. Then one day I was on the 104 bus that goes down Broadway and a woman got on bus. I said, "Hey you're the accordion player in that klezmer band that plays in front of Zabar's." She knew me because she took piano lessons with the wife of the bassoon player in my woodwind quintet. She said to me, "We're looking for a clarinet player for my klezmer band." She thought I was going to recommend a friend or a student. But the words came out of my mouth like I was in a trance. I said to her: "I'd like to try." And that's how the whole klezmer adventure all began for me.

The great New Orleans clarinetists like Bechet, Barney Bigard and Johnny Dodds had a very distinctive punch to their playing and I found Tarras' approach to sound production to be similar (within his own specific genre).

As I mentioned before, growing up I never thought about (or had much exposure to) klezmer. That was the music of my great grandparents. Based on what little I heard, I appreciated it and thought it was intriguing, but I didn't get into it deeply.

However, in the mid-80s something started to happen when Gorbachev was in power in the former Soviet Union: glasnost and perestroika. Eastern Europe (that I always thought of as being behind the "Iron Curtain") was starting to open up. I'm not a sociologist or historian, but it seemed to me that with that opening and sociological/political shift, people in general started to look at Eastern Europe in a different way and Jews globally started to reconnect to their Jewish heritage.

I also started getting curious about my own Eastern European-ness and was beginning to subconsciously gravitate towards the music of my ancestry. So the experiences of having heard Tarras in 1980, reading books by authors like Milan Kundera and Bruno Schultz, and going to concerts at the Balkan Arts Center with concerts of music from all over Eastern Europe started to connect the dots for me. I also thought about my connection with jazz and my love of playing non-notated music.

I thought klezmer could make sense as a kind of musical home. Even in a very unformed way at the time I felt instinctively like I could bring my heritage and my roots together with my love of improvisation. When I decided to get into klezmer and started playing in this modest little band, I said to myself that I'd just be doing it for fun, play at weddings and parties and connect more with my own Jewishness. It was incredible to go into neighborhoods in Brooklyn to play and meet Yiddish speakers who still retained the language. I thought that only Chassidim spoke Yiddish, so it was astonishing to meet people of my generation and a little older who hadn't lost that part of their cultural heritage.

I did these modest little gigs for about a year until a band called The Klezmatics heard about me and asked me to come to Europe. At that time the first klezmer revival (that went from approximately the mid-70s- early '80s) had basically run its course. The focus of that movement was to regain this lost art form by copying the old klezmer records and learning from as many surviving older practitioners as they could. But in the late '80s there was a new vibe starting to form along with all the sociological changes that I mentioned previously. The Klezmatics came to the music with a whole new attitude. As a band we embraced improvisation. We wanted to create original material based on the older forms and we played super amplified. I thought of us as a kind of a Jewish punk band. When we went to Germany to play festivals, the place was filled with dancing, screaming, partying Europeans. That was quite a rush.

I recorded with The Klezmatics in December 1990 on the German label Piranha and many would say that the second klezmer revival was really born with that recording at that moment. We embraced the avant garde and at the same time approached the music from a pop perspective. We were doing something quite new and it was a super exciting time. I made two major recordings with The Klezmatics: "Rhythm and Jews" and "Jews with Horns." Together with The Klezmatics I was also part of a collaboration with Itzhak Perlman and several major klezmer bands that included a recording and a PBS special. It was quite a fantastic run, but in the mid-90s I left The Klezmatics to go out on my own as a leader and soloist.

A couple of interesting things happened right around the time when I decided to pursue a solo career. In the mid-90s, the composer Osvaldo Golijov and the Kronos Quartet invited me to record "The Dreams and Prayers of Isaac the Blind," a 35-minute piece for klezmer clarinet and string quartet. It became a very important recording for me. Also, at that time John Zorn invited me to do the very first recording on the radical Jewish culture line of his new label Tzadik. I did my very first recording under my own name, "Klezmer Madness," plus a subsequent recording for Tzadik called "Klezmer New York." For that second album I composed a suite of music that described an imaginary meeting in New York City between Sidney Bechet and the klezmer giant Naftule Brandwein; and it's still one of my favorite recordings. I put together a kind of musical portrait of these two musicians, Bechet and Brandwein (one African American and one Eastern European Jewish) in the same room, jamming. It was a metaphor for all improv I've done and all the worlds I knew, putting them into one big "soup." That was the real start for me as a band leader and a composer of my own originals.

What was the biggest challenge in learning it, especially regarding technique?

I had a background in jazz and off-the-page playing. However, there is a very specific sound in klezmer that's not obvious or easy to get. If I hear somebody play klezmer who hasn't really integrated the specific style and sound, I can tell if they're a classical player or if they're a jazz player because I can hear it in their sound.

It was a challenge for me to really get a correct klezmer sound. It took thousands of hours of study. Technically speaking, I found that if I used another mouthpiece that would help me obtain the timbre, volume and intensity that I wanted and needed. When I recorded with Kronos Quartet, I was thinking that since the piece we were doing was written by a classical composer it would be best to use my classical mouthpiece. But when we did a test recording and listened back, I knew the sound wasn't right. So I put the klezmer mouthpiece back on. As soon as we started recording again the quartet looked at me and said "man, that's amazing!" It became clear to me in that moment that I had truly found my own sound. It was a big lesson for me.

Another important aspect I discovered is that the groove of the music should be contained inside the sound. Even playing a single lined instrument, you should be able to make people dance all by yourself, with no rhythm section. It's all about the inflection and the subtle dynamics.

For every great jazz player that I love I believe that's true as well. For example, when you hear the two great tenor players of the late 30s' Basie band Lester Young and Herschel Evans, they each had totally different approaches, but both of those guys could make you levitate out of your chair. The sense of swing and groove is embedded in their sound. I think that's the goal in great klezmer too. At the heart of it, both genres of music were initially created to interact with dancers, so having a super danceable melodic line is crucial.

Since klezmer doesn't rely on improv the way jazz does, how do you get inside the music and make it your own?

When I was first learning klezmer, it was pointed out to me that it was more like Baroque music with a melody to be ornamented and decorated. It's interesting that early jazz players like Buster Bailey said that when they were playing, they never called it improvisation, but rather called it ornamentation.

In klezmer, the main thing to do with the dance melodies is to embellish them. But in terms of improvisation, there are different kinds of pieces that feature a monophonic/melismatic line with a drone underneath. One of these is called a "doina" which is a sort of cross between a Romanian shepherd's song and cantorial singing. It's very melodic with a lot of flurries and different kinds of decoration, plus you also have the ornament called a "krekhts"– a catch in the voice, a sob, a squeeze – which basically creates the plaintive quality of the music.

When I first got into developing a system of improvisation in klezmer, I started by copying old doinas. Naftule Brandwein and Dave Tarras both used a whole vocabulary of standard "licks" so initially I simply copied those from old recordings from the 1920s-50s and tried to assimilate those into my playing. But then I said to myself maybe I can add some of the stuff I'm experimenting with, like alternate fingerings (inspired by Coltrane, Lester Young, Bechet, etc.). I didn't want to simply paste jazz on top of klezmer so I was looking for something more integrated.

I worked very hard to retain the essence of what the old klezmer musicians were playing and then mixed that with my own sounds. I never wanted to go and take 78 rpm records and copy them note for note as an end goal for performance. For me, that was just the starting point.

What were some of your most exciting projects?

In the early 2000s I asked the Canadian producer and multi-instrumentalist Socalled to become a featured artist with my band at the time, "Klezmer Madness." He was a real pioneer in terms of bringing hip-hop into klezmer music. We produced the album "Bubbemeisis" together and later formed the group Abraham Inc. in 2006. For that project we invited Fred Wesley, the legendary master funk trombonist and arranger (James Brown, Parliament etc.). We still tour when we can. It's a fantastic Jewish/African American dance party.

I'm also doing a large-scale collaboration with Kathleen Tagg, a great pianist and composer. The project is called "Breath and Hammer" which combines clarinet with a whole "piano orchestra" made up of loops and samples. Kathleen and I are also writing a clarinet concerto together which will be premiered with the Santa Rosa Symphony in November 2021.

Talk about your work in France.

When I was 20, I lived in France and became fluent in French. I stayed one year and went back to the US in 1977. Then in 1999, over 20 years later, I got invited to play at a festival in Amiens where I was approached by numerous journalists. They were a bit shy about speaking in English, so I ended up giving four hours of interviews in French. It was amazing that I retained the language after all those years, and that ended up being very important for me in terms of having a career in France! Right after that concert the record label *Tag Bleu* invited me to work with them and I met my French agent, and I've been on that French journey ever since. It's been fantastic that France has really "adopted me". People often stop me on the street in Paris and say "David, your music has changed my life." That's so gratifying to me.

How did COVID affect your music?

All of our touring was cancelled, so we did a lot of projects online. The new project I'm creating with Kathleen Tagg as a producer and player is something we call a "Mazel Tov Cocktail Party" and was first launched as part of an online residency at Brandeis University. The title came from a comment from a Trump supporter during the 2016 election. They were talking about the rapper JZ who supported Hillary, saying, "Did you see that degenerate throwing MAZEL TOV cocktails at the police in his music video?" (They meant of course to say Molotov cocktails.) I found that incredibly amusing! The project takes that comment and turns it on his head as a good-vibes explosion to celebrate our shared humanity.

During lockdown we created eight little music videos where each musician was filmed in front of green screens. The incredible filmmaker Michael McQuilken stitched it all together, and we had our amazing multicultural band (that had never physically met) all in the same virtual room. We are continuing that project with plans for live touring and the release of our videos, including a crazy square dance with a rap in the middle of it.

The connection for me with klezmer is an emotional one and a sense of rootedness with my family. It morphs and mutates into other different things. I'm very proud of my Jewishness and consider myself a person who invites people into my world, not living in the "fortress" of my own culture. It's about tolerance, inclusion and trying to bring people together.

AARON KULA

Aaron Kula is the music director and accordionist with the Klezmer Company Jazz Orchestra, which he founded in 1997. He resides in Boston, Massachusetts.

Did you grow up listening to klezmer?

My father was a cantor, conductor and musicologist. We had Jewish music playing in our home all the time. I grew up listening to cantorial music, Chassidic melodies and klezmer music. I always wanted to play the music I heard in our home.

You founded the KCJO in 1997. What did you feel was the best way to bring the music from Eastern Europe to the world in a way that people would fall in love with it?

I started performing the standard klezmer and Yiddish melodies with a seven-piece band. We began playing loosely improvised arrangements that took us weeks to organize. Then we wanted more formal structures so I started arranging klezmer tunes for a nine-piece band. Our trumpeter was familiar with Latin rhythms and then we started fusing them and jazz harmonies with klezmer and Yiddish tunes. This led to very polished orchestrations with a new spin.

What shared energies do you see between Jewish folk music and jazz?

Both traditions share the basic concept that music should elicit joy and movement, specifically dance.

If you had to give one main reason you enjoy creating, leading and performing klezmer, would you say it's for the melodies, rhythm, or the larger picture of its historical context?

I think it is more of a basic and fundamental feeling that it makes you happy. Of course, the genre connects to my heritage so that is certainly a motivation to create new interpretations for an old tradition.

Why do you think as an artform that it has survived from the 1800s?

The artform connects cultures and generations while allowing the freedom to express musical influences of geography and the next generation.

What are some of your favorite songs and why?

My favorite songs are the ones I perform. There are thousands and it would be impossible to pick even a few of my favorites. They are all my favorites.

Other comments?

The ultimate sound of any klezmer music is a result of the personnel that performs it. Therefore, each ensemble will offer their own version of the music even if it is the same tune. That's what makes the genre really interesting and vibrant.

PHILIPPE LAYE

Composer, saxophone and clarinet player, leader and teacher Philippe Laye plays in the Tzigish Trio. He's based in Côte d'Azur, France. He can be reached at klezmer84@gmail.com. (From left are Frédéric Besozzi (violin); Sylvain Gargalian (accordion); and Philippe Laye. Photo c. Cecile Aubry.

How did you first learn about klezmer?

I discovered klezmer music in 1998 when I was a student in Paris at the music conservatory, a very nice discovery!

Klezmer music brings me back to the history of shtetls that existed in Eastern Europe. Immigrants brought this music to the USA. Klezmer also allowed me to become interested in religion and therefore to play in synagogues for weddings or bar mitzvahs.

Why it has survived and made it through different "waves"?

Because this music speaks to our soul. It is sometimes very sad and very joyful like gypsy music.

I also like Oriental consonances and the Romanian *doina*, which gives place to improvisation like jazz. The basis of klezmer is not improvisation but rather melody.

Do you feel the interest in it continues to intensify?

In France, few bands play klezmer music, but since 2000, we love klezmer and the number of bands is increasing. A lot of clarinet teachers like to give klezmer music to their students, and there are more klezmer pieces being published in France.

What are some of your favorite songs?

Certainly "Yiddishe Momme" and "Oy Yossel Yossel."

Talk about how it feels to play it.

I like and have played many times in a synagogue. It's different from a concert hall. The emotions are different. There is a beautiful Jewish music festival at the synagogue in Carpentras [France] and it is very popular with the public! Music animates my soul and has accompanied me since my childhood.

Debbie Burke

My passion for klezmer music and Eastern European music has led me to edit tunes that I particularly appreciate with two musician friends. My four books, "Klezmer, Gipsy, Armenian Music - 12 Pieces for Solo Clarinet;" "Klezmer, Gipsy, Armenian Music - 12 Pieces for Solo Violin;" "Klezmer, Gipsy, Armenian Music - 9 Pieces for Solo Clarinet;" and "Klezmer, Gipsy, Armenian Music, 9 Pieces for Solo Violin" allow musicians, clarinetists or violinists (amateurs or professionals), to learn or improve in the art of this captivating music.

LORI LIPPITZ

Lori Lippitz is the founder of Maxwell Street Klezmer Band and the _Klezmer Music Foundation,_ and a cantorial soloist.

How did you become interested in klezmer?

I was always closely connected to the Jewish community through my family's strong cultural ties. But klezmer music gave me a way of doing something for the Jewish community that wasn't only synagogue- or Israel-centered. Not that there's anything wrong with that!

Do you feel that klezmer reflects either a social, political, historical or spiritual sensibility?

Klezmer music reflects a spiritual sensibility most of all, since it is primarily derived from Chassidic nigunim. There are background connections in those other realms, but objectively, the music expresses Chassidic fervor and drives dancing.

As a cantor, what can you say about the connection between music and faith; how does klezmer dovetail with Judaism?

As a cantorial soloist, the connection for me is that the voice of the Old World cantor that can be heard in klezmer music: Singing *mitn krekhtz* (with a cry in the voice), imploring, expressing the pain and hardships of His people and seeking divine aid. The music is an emotional time capsule. In it, I can hear the living, expressive voices of my own ancestors. Although klezmer music is not liturgical, it is very spiritual, and playing klezmer music has been the gateway into the Jewish community for many musicians whom I know and work with, both professional and amateur.

Music and faith are connected because both of them occupy a level of emotional reality that is not tied to logic or reason. Klezmer music – for those who remember it from their youth – connects the heart with the past in a similar way that the smell of latkes brings back memories of family, festivals and childhood. Klezmer is the "soul music" of Ashkenazic Judaism and expresses our collective cultural experience. Concrete example: The majority of students in my Junior Klezmer Orchestra come from Russian-speaking homes, where the love of Yiddishkeit is a much stronger connection to Judaism than religious belief or synagogue affiliation.

Why do you think as an artform that it has survived?

When I discovered klezmer music in the late 1970s (thanks to an early California revival band and a folk music show on a Chicago classical music radio station), it spoke to me much more deeply than the Jewish music I had been raised on. I immediately identified with the emotional authenticity of the shtetl melodies and style, and was especially taken with the confluence of klezmer and early American jazz found in 78 rpm recordings. I think it has survived because it strikes other people as it strikes me, as an authentic and enduring expression of a lost community (lost to the Holocaust, but also to assimilation).

Musically, how would you characterize ebb and flow of interest in klezmer over the years?

The "klezmer wave" (mid-80s to mid-90s) has come and gone, but it seeded communities around the world with hundreds of little bands and ensembles that continue playing and evolving. For example, my band used to play in Europe in the 1990s and 2000s, returning seven times to Germany and Austria. But now, they have their own local orchestras and don't need to "import" us (although we have an invitation to return in 2022).

What are some of your favorite songs in klezmer?

Technically, klezmer is instrumental music, and songs are Yiddish folk and theater music. My favorite klezmer instrumental recordings from the 1920s include those from Lt. Joseph Frankel, Abe Schwartz and all of the early Dave Tarras and Naftule Brandwein recordings. Out of contemporary groups, I always have a soft spot in my heart for my first exposure to klezmer with "The Klezmorim." My favorite Yiddish performances are by Molly Picon and Aaron Lebedeff.

Talk about the sense of community and playing with others.

COVID notwithstanding... In 1983, I started Maxwell Street Klezmer Band with a dream of replacing DJs at Jewish weddings and bar mitzvah parties with klezmer music. The band's impact has been significant. We've played about 1,300 bar/bat mitzvah parties in 37 years, and we hope to resume shortly. In 1994, I started a not-for-profit, the Klezmer Music Foundation, to get support for the community-based projects I wanted to build. These include the Junior Klezmer Orchestra (running continuously since 1994), several adult synagogue klezmer bands, an English-language klezmer theater project (The Yiddish Arts Ensemble), and an interfaith group called the Salaam-Shalom Music Project. All of these ensembles, professional or grassroots, bring together musicians in a way that is warm and familial, and bring together the community at large with music at its core.

What are klezmer audiences looking for?

The quality of the professional ensemble performances, and the excitement of belonging to one of the community bands.

There is a particular need in the non-coastal cities and towns of American (not East or West Coast) to revive Yiddish and klezmer music. Sometimes, the revival seems to swirl around New York, while it is really needed in the heartland. That is what I have tried to do.

ALEXANDRE LITWAK

Alexandre Litwak *is an arranger who plays clarinet and alto sax in Gefilte Swing, which he founded in 1999. He's based in Paris.*

How did you get into clarinet and sax, and what was your first performance?

There were nearly two generations between me and my parents. I was born in 1970 and experienced the 1920s/30s/40s thanks to them. I heard a lot of swing and New Orleans jazz recordings, but also a lot of classical music (Debussy, Ravel, Poulenc). I first heard Bix Beiderbecke and Sidney Bechet recordings when I was 15 years old – it was like a revolution in my head! I wanted to play the cornet but it was too difficult to play so many notes with only three pistons! So thanks to Bechet, I chose clarinet.

My first lessons were at a private jazz school, but my teacher was ignorant of any jazz pre-bebop. I quit after ten lessons and started learning directly from the recordings. I then studied with a classical clarinet teacher who really taught me how to play the instrument, even though he knew I was not headed for a classical career!

After several years I purchased a saxophone – a C Melody sax (like Frankie Trumbauer). But it was not tuned to more modern instruments so I switched to alto saxophone and also some baritone sax. I even tried the cornet again. It wasn't as difficult as I had remembered, but learning clarinet and trumpet at the same time was not easy. Not everyone can be Benny Carter. I had to choose – my father who was a dentist warned me that my teeth would not survive the trumpet.

I was 18 years old when I first performed with only three years of clarinet experience, not to mention that I was also going to school during those years. And with my friends at that school, we formed a small jazz band with a string bass, percussion, guitar, trombone and myself, and we played every Saturday night at a local bar. We didn't make much money but the drinks were on the house and the girls would be watching us. I've kept some recordings from those days. Just awful!

How does your knowledge about different cultures and languages help you to be a better musician?

Debbie Burke

Although my name is synonymous with a Yiddish accent, no one ever spoke Yiddish with me. I never spoke it as I knew about 50 words or so. And my English isn't much better. What really helped me to become a better musician was the enormous mass of recordings that our predecessors left for us, as much in klezmer as swing. Be inspired by others, copy them and add something of yourself. Recordings from the past and the present are our étude books. And don't forget that klezmer and swing are music that came from our oral traditions.

Talk about your latest CD and your favorite tracks.

Six years had passed since our last CD (2012-2018) and the time had come to make a new CD. Our sound and style had evolved, and new players brought their own standards, fresh ideas and a new approach. This CD is also an homage to my father who passed away in June 2017 at the age of 95. Although not a musician himself, he never stopped supporting me and encouraging me in all my musical endeavors. He was enthusiastic each time I announced a concert, a private event or a festival where Gefilte Swing performed. And he was proud that the orchestra that I founded in 1999 was still active. His determination is also mine, to continue with this group, regardless of the inevitable and unpredictable changes that life may bring.

I chose these tunes based on the sounds that would have been close to those my father had listened to and loved; the atmosphere that he had transmitted to me with enthusiasm that I wanted to recreate, without being afraid of adding other sounds.

Every tune on this album is my favorite – each one telling a short story, whether true or false. Imagine that Benny Goodman had replaced Naftule Brandwein, or Sidney Bechet playing a John Zorn composition...etc.

Why did you choose this as a band name?

I grew up in a so-called "mixed" family. My mother wasn't Jewish. I wanted to create a mixture between swing and klezmer. I figured that taking part of the name of this dish so familiar to Jews would be perfect for this music. Wouldn't you agree that we are playing a sort of "stuffed swing"? I always think that you play as the person you are.

Why did you choose to work with the other musicians?

I don't like to play music all by myself and I don't see myself as a "sideman." What's important to me is the group, otherwise I wouldn't have called this "Gefilte Swing" but "Alexandre Litwak Sextet." Even if I'm the leader, I wanted, for example, to include a trumpet, which is more of a lead instrument than the clarinet. I also wanted an accordion and a tuba to emphasize the "trad" side. Each player came with his musical past and brought a personal touch and knowledge.

What is the most important thing to know about klezmer as a musician? As a music lover?

Klezmer is festive music that has drawn on many other types of music. It's music that has traveled from Europe to America and back again to Europe. To play the way we do in the Gefilte Swing, you need to understand this and not get locked into a single approach.

What are you working on now?

I'm working on myself!

What do you love most about being a musician?

Making our audience dream.

Other comments?

For klezmer musicians, I'm a swing musician; for swing musicians, I'm a klezmer musician... Jews don't consider me as a fellow Jew, but for non-Jews, I'm Jewish. Whatever! You always need to find your path and stick to it...that's what I try to do, with what I am.

Translation by Susan Vaillant

ALLISON and WAYNE MARKS

Authors, "Benny Feldman's All-Star Klezmer Band"(Green Bean Books).

What is your muse when you write in general and specifically for this book?

As a writing team, we share a similar muse when approaching any children's book, whether it's a 32-page picture book or a middle-grade novel. We put ourselves in the minds of our readers and ask questions that drive our decision-making about characterization and plotting: *What are the kinds of things that interest kids today? What do they worry about? What will make them laugh out loud? What will keep them turning the page?*

When our twins were younger (they're now in their late 20s), we used to tell them impromptu stories before bedtime—wild, off-the-cuff tales that would have them in fits of giggles and begging for more. These memories serve as muses, reminding us that even at a young age, children understand devices like irony and exaggeration; they comprehend the value of a sympathetic protagonist and a wicked villain; and they find satisfaction in watching characters grow and change. Watching their reactions as these stories unfolded was revelatory and, to this day, serves as a basis for how we write for this audience.

When outlining how we would approach *Benny Feldman's All-Star Klezmer Band*, we answered the *What do children worry about?* question by focusing on universal issues that have affected middle-school students from time immemorial: fitting in, bullying, fractured friendships, crushes and the general insecurities that come from simply surviving perhaps the most awkward of all circumstances—being an eleven-year-old.

To position Benny, our book's fiddling hero, outside of the mainstream, we made him passionate about klezmer—a genre of music shared by no one else at his school in the fictional town of Ardmore, Ohio. Then we gave him the task of recruiting fellow classmates to join his band to compete in a talent show. All of the ensuing drama and laughter flow from this challenge. Along the way, we repeatedly asked ourselves, *what would have kept our own children engaged in the story?*

Your book touches on inclusion and creativity. Why?

One of the main themes of the book is "How all music is connected . . . and how music connects us all." We began writing in 2017, a time of great political division in the United States and, for that matter, the world. We thought it was important to write about a topic that unites us rather than separates us; namely, the universality of music.

The Highland Square neighborhood in Akron, where we have lived for over 30 years, hosts an amazing event known as *PorchRokr*, in which more than a hundred bands of all types perform in hour-long sets. It has grown into a massively attended event where people of all ages, races and backgrounds gather for a day that can best be described as "pure joy." Wayne's Irish rock band often plays at this event. The real magic is walking throughout the neighborhood and listening to the diverse sounds drifting from porch to porch. It nourishes one's soul to witness music's power to bring people together. The annual gathering also served as inspiration for Benny's range of musical interests, which run the gamut from klezmer to didgeridoo. Benny's band is a microcosm of this diversity: a Jewish fiddler; Jennifer, a jazz-loving drummer; Royce, an African-American classically trained clarinet prodigy; and Stewart, an accordion player from Cajun country. In one scene, Benny's violin mentor, Uncle Maxwell, has the band try different instruments from diverse cultures before teaching them about the expressions of happiness and sorrow which lie at the heart of klezmer, and, indeed, all music. Perhaps one of our reviewers said it best: "The book is a love letter to music."

As for the creativity aspect of *Benny Feldman's All-Star Klezmer Band* and our other books, we have noticed many middle-grade novels with male protagonists that revolve around sports. While a worthy topic, our goal is to celebrate children who gravitate toward artistic and scientific pursuits. The challenge is infusing these stories with the same level of tension and excitement that keep the pages turning.

How do you think this will speak to children of different cultures and religious backgrounds?

From our initial conversations about the book, we were committed to writing a story that both highlights an integral part of Jewish culture and speaks to every reader. Benny's typical middle-grade angst cuts across all cultures and backgrounds. We believe Benny's story of overcoming stage fright and his love of music is a universal one. Additionally, any child who has ever felt like a "fish out of water" or, in Benny's word, "weird," will immediately find a kindred spirit in the book's titular character.

The story should particularly resonate with adventurous students who are musically inclined, regardless of their background. In our author's note, we encourage readers to take their own musical journey by listening to the many compositions scattered throughout the text (e.g., Dave Brubeck Quartet's "Blue Rondo à la Turk," Maurice Ravel's "Kaddish," klezmer tunes, etc.). We are confident that budding fiddlers and clarinetists will be floored by the level of virtuosity displayed by the klezmer greats.

What did you enjoy most about the process of writing this book? What was the greatest challenge?

Let's start with the greatest challenge. Writing about music isn't easy, even if you're a seasoned player. Wayne has played the fiddle in various bands for 25 years, so he could lend authenticity to the troubles and triumphs of learning to gel as a group, the arguments that arise when deciding on an arrangement, and the elation that comes when everything clicks. But writing about what music *sounds* like can often feel like trying to describe "red" to someone who is colorblind. When addressing the uninitiated (we assumed most readers would be unfamiliar with klezmer), how does one describe a glissando or a *krekht* (klezmer moaning sound), or a *doina*, the improvised lament that often precedes the jauntier part of a tune?

We turned to figurative language when all else failed. To Benny's best friend, Ollie, a klezmer tune playing from an old 78 record sounds like "feral cats fighting in a burlap sack." For Benny, it is a "chorus of angels." The glissando at the beginning of *Rhapsody in Blue* is "an express elevator going from the lobby to the top floor of a skyscraper in three seconds." When Benny plays a solo near the end of the novel, we wrote: "The sound of mourning hung like a low rain crowd over the auditorium." Ultimately, we understand that words fail to do justice to the music. Thankfully, there's YouTube to fill in the details.

The answer to what we enjoyed most is easy—writing together. We laugh, we debate, we redline, we get *verklempt* after reading a passage that moves us to tears. We are incredibly fortunate to have each other to bounce ideas off of. When the finished book arrives, there is no sweeter feeling than knowing we took the journey side by side. For this book, writing with klezmer tunes booming in the background was another joyful perk. We highly recommend it, no matter what you're writing about (or if you're writing at all)!

When did you first learn about klezmer? What do you enjoy about the music and what are some of your favorite songs and artists?

As the musician in the family, Wayne has known about traditional Jewish music since his youth, but he didn't take an interest in klezmer until he began playing in bands. He introduced the tune "Tantz, Tantz, Yiddelech" (*Dance, Dance, Jews*) to the bluegrass band he played with for years. It is featured prominently in the book as the tune Benny's band plays at the talent show.

The book includes several other of our favorites (too numerous to mention here) from early recordings by Abe Schwartz's Orchestra to modern performances by The Klezmatics. Mickey Katz (noted parodist and jazz clarinetist) is also mentioned. His music was revived in the excellent album, *Don Byron Plays the Music of Mickey Katz*. For an encore, Benny's band performs "Bei Mir Bistu Sheyn," easily the most famous klezmer tune. Our favorite version is from the Klezmer Conservatory Band album, *Jumping Night in the Garden of Eden*, 1988. Not mentioned in the book, but at the top of our list is

Andy Statman's "Flatbush Waltz" which Wayne would play on his mandolin for inspiration.

Our feelings about klezmer can be summed up by the character of Jennifer, who says when first listening to a tune played by The Klezmatics, "It totally kicks, B-Man. A real challenge, too. Who wouldn't like this?" Within the span of a few minutes, a klezmer tune can express the full range of human emotions, from the depths of despair to the heights of jubilation. It can be infectious, heartbreaking, and, if done correctly for its intended purpose (dancing), exhausting.

NAMI MELUMAD

Nami Melumad is an Israeli-Dutch composer for film, TV, games and media. She's based in Los Angeles, California.

What was your early musical training like?

Growing up in Israel, I studied piano and flute. I joined a couple of youth orchestras and ensembles and mainly played classical music. As a teenager, I picked up a guitar and taught myself how to play, and started composing some songs. Around that time, I began to develop an interest in film music. I used to play my favorite movie-themes on the piano, study them and develop thematic material on my own. I took music and chemistry in high school and had a great opportunity to write a musical for our music group, which we then performed live on stage. That drew me even closer to storytelling. My first job out of school was writing music for theater, and I greatly enjoyed how music can influence emotion and help shape the story and the director's vision.

After my military service and a long trip to New Zealand and Australia, I was admitted to the Jerusalem Academy of Music. They let me skip the first year which was a great boost of confidence. I majored in Interdisciplinary Composition, from traditional counterpoint and orchestration to jazz harmony, big band arrangements, ethnic music, writing for contemporary dance and film. During my time there, I scored anything I could get my hands on: shorts, animations, documentaries, web series, PSAs. I went on another backpacking trip to China and Thailand before moving to Los Angeles in August 2014 to take the graduate scoring program at USC. This program provided incredible insights into the way Hollywood composers work and how stressful their schedules can be. I worked on as many student films as possible, I think it was about 15 projects in total. USC also introduced music department roles such as copying, music preparation and orchestration, which helped me make a living in LA after school.

How did you become involved in "American Pickle"?

I pitched for the project back in November 2018. My agent at the Gorfaine/Schwartz agency, Maria Machado, called and asked me to put together a reel for it (a Jewish immigrant composing a film about a Jewish immigrant seemed like a pretty good match!).

Luckily, I had samples from previous projects. I also wrote a couple of cues during that weekend and asked my cousin, Ran Kampel, to record the clarinet part with his iPhone, guerilla-style. A few weeks after I got a call from her and composer Michael Giacchino, whose music I grew up adoring. It's the kind of call you get only in your dreams. I still feel it's completely surreal to work with him. He pitched the idea of us collaborating on "An American Pickle," and then we met for lunch and the rest is history. After the first spotting session, he composed the main themes, and I crafted the entire score. I feel incredibly fortunate for this experience.

How has the project furthered your own understanding of the music?

Yes, of course, I feel every visual project expands my own cinematic language which consequently deepens my understanding of music. When you use music to support a story, to enhance the edit, to shape a scene or a montage sequence with pace (tempo), tone and color, it's a lot about exploring your thematic materials. Sometimes you'd be surprised about the variations and textures you can go to. It's incredible where a picture can take you. This project in particular presented an incredible opportunity to bring Jewish music to the front. Klezmer styles haven't been much used in the film scoring world before. How many Hollywood films feature a Jewish score? You have "Yentl," "Schindler's List" and... that's about it. I was excited to bring Jewish music to the front. And what I mean by that is that it's not entirely klezmer; it's a matchmaking scenario between the Jewish elements and the full orchestra that provides the entire dynamic range of emotions.

You could hear influences of Israeli songs, Eastern European harmonies and melodies, and certain instruments that aren't often featured like clarinet and violin solos in klezmer style, and balalaika and tambourine to name a few but it's all combined into the cinematic-fantastical feel of a modern-day film score.

We only had one scene where it was full-on klezmer music, and even then, I utilized the full emotional range that the orchestra provided. The score took it over the top, which made the scene much funnier.

This project also furthered my understanding of building up to a climax. The scene at the synagogue towards the end of the movie is actually one of the scenes I scored early on. From the perspective of character development, you have Herschel who knows who he is but having been "pickled" from 2019, he's a fish out of the water and doesn't know what the world is in 2019. His identity, however, is that Jewish representation I'm talking about, combined with full epic orchestral moments when he (spoiler alert!) escapes the Cossacks, builds his massive pickle empire, etc. Herschel's musical world is very different from Ben's world, which was a little more modern and millennial, so if you follow his underscore, it's very minimal and not super Jewish. There are some woodwinds but almost no strings.

We have some drums and a guitar. And it slowly builds to that scene in the synagogue with both Herschel that Ben gets the bigger orchestral treatment because it's such an emotional climax. Having that instrumentation grow through the movie is something that helps the audience understand Ben's development and arc to deal with his grief and re-accept himself and his own identity.

What was it like to write for this movie? The biggest challenge, the most fun?

Writing for this movie was such a thriller for me, both in terms of the movie itself, which I felt speaks to me personally on so many levels (being Jewish, millennial, immigrant, and a soda-stream addict), and in terms of the scoring process. I can't stress enough how much I learned from this experience, the feedback sessions with Michael and Brandon Trost (the director).

I guess the biggest challenge was stepping into very big shoes. When you're working with an A-list composer like Michael Giacchino, there's a certain expectation. It's a pretty high standard. I was always confident about my work, but up until that point in time, I have never worked on a project of this scale. Taking a four-and-a-half-minute piece and turning it into 68 minutes of the score was a challenge in and of itself. And because of that animated quality of the film, I knew that the score has a major role to fill also in terms of emotion. Luckily, I think it all worked out.

The most fun part was the three days we spent at Fox Newman Scoring Stage with the orchestra, who did an absolutely fantastic job recording the score to picture.

Josh Rantz took the clarinet parts to a whole new level – he's just an absolutely phenomenal performer. Belinda Broughton on violin brought so much soul to the score as well. Mixing with Dennis Sands at his studio was another dream come true for me. And then, Michael – I have such deep love and appreciation for him. He's the best, and I'm so fortunate to have him in my life. Just thinking about the whole experience now fills my heart with joy. "An American Pickle" brought so many wonderful people into my life and I'm super grateful for all of it.

What is the appeal of klezmer: for yourself and for audiences?

When I think of klezmer music, I instantly feel a beat and a drive to dance. It's fun, but the truth is there are so many different styles, tempos, feels and ensembles that exist within this genre. What's fascinating to me is that klezmer borrows elements from other musical styles, often influenced by the country of origin, and these blends make it even more relatable.

From the perspective of film scoring, klezmer suggests many opportunities for expression. Outside of that, quick, exciting upbeat tunes, especially when combined with a full orchestra. When you break down what's in the music – the melodies, the motives, the harmony (or chord progression), individual instrumentation – you see that you can utilize this genre in a wide and wild range of emotions.

What are you doing musically today?

After "An American Pickle," Michael and I collaborated on the virtual reality video game, *Medal of Honor: Above and Beyond,* for which we recently won Best Score for a Video Game from the International Film Music Critiques Association (IFMCA). I'm currently scoring "Star Trek: Prodigy" for Nickelodeon, and a limited series for Netflix (which I can't name yet). Also, the documentary short I recently scored, "Colette," was just nominated for an Academy Award!

I also serve as a board member for the Alliance for Women Film Composers. We advocate for gender parity in the scoring world.

HANKUS NETSKY

Another icon and widely acclaimed figure in the contemporary klezmer scene is Dr. Hankus Netsky, the founder and director of the Klezmer Conservatory Band, and Co-chair, Contemporary Improvisation Department, New England Conservatory.

Was your initial attraction to klezmer because you grew up listening to it, or did your musical or spiritual exploration bring you there?

My grandfather and five uncles played it. I didn't grow up listening to it because it was out of favor while I was growing up but I knew that it existed and occasionally heard some of them play it. When I was nineteen, I started bugging them to teach me to play it.

How do you feel that the style reflects either a social, political, historical or spiritual sensibility?

It has a spiritual sensibility that imbues all of Eastern European Jewish culture. It's apolitical (unlike a lot of other Jewish music) which is why it's a unifying force.

Why do you play it today?

I play it today as one of many types of music that I play, but I get a lot of work in that genre and have been pigeonholed a bit as a "klezmer musician." I play saxophone, piano, accordion, clarinet and oboe.

What are the variations within the genre?

Klezmer is the repertoire of the Eastern European Jewish folk instrumentalist. Related genres include Yiddish folksong, Yiddish theater music, Hassidic music, cantorial music and Yiddish art song but to some extent klezmorim might play repertoire from any of those genres.

Are there techniques specific to the genre you had to learn?

Everything about it. It's all of the sounds of the Eastern European Yiddish and Ashkenazic Hebrew world as they sound on instruments.

Why do you think as an artform that it has survived?

Because it's an artistic virtuosic tradition. All Eastern European Jewish genres had been largely discarded by the 1960s because pretty much every major influential Jewish figure of the last hundred or so years (Herzl, Schechter, Kaplan, Benderly, Berkson, Ben Gurion, etc.) had mistakenly decided that Eastern European Jewish culture was a "transitional" culture that was a thing of the past. As a leader of the resurgence, I can tell you that you can't extinguish any great culture, even if you're trying to advance a political agenda that has no room for it. Eventually it comes back and this one's here to stay. Even if the mainstream Jewish community hasn't even vaguely caught up with that idea, the rest of the world has embraced it.

Have you been aware of more interest in it recently?

Interest is always growing as mainstream Jewish organizations continue to promote rootless banal musical expression.

What are some of your favorite songs and why?

It's a performative tradition, not about the tunes but the way the great players play them. Brandwein, Tarras, Joseph Moskowitz, Joseph Hoffman and H. Steiner are some of the great artists of the genre.

Talk about the sense of community. Why do you like playing klezmer as part of an ensemble?

It's great to bring people together to something with artistic merit and ancestral roots that was casually discarded, especially when it was discarded out of self-hatred. King David said it best in Psalm 118: *The stone that was discarded has become the chief cornerstone.* The Jews have done that a lot, apparently even in building their first temple!

LAURA ROSENBERG

"Myrna Oy" is the Yiddish cabaret alter ego of musician and arts administrator Laura Rosenberg.

When did you get introduced to klezmer and why does it inspire you?

Like many North American Ashkenazic Jews of my generation, I heard a little klezmer and Yiddish music at community events, and a good bit more on records played by older family members. It always inspired joy and a craving to "dance along," and seemed inextricably linked to my cultural experience of being Jewish. During my student years, I even had the opportunity to study briefly with the legendary Yiddish singer Martha

Schlamme, whose recordings had been particularly influential in my childhood. As a young professional musician, though, I was so focused on my classical choral conducting career that it never occurred to me to pursue klezmer or Yiddish music as a performer.

What was your first public performance as a vocalist?

I joke that my midlife crisis arrived in the form of an irresistible compulsion to sing in Yiddish, but that's pretty much the truth. At the time, I was running a classical music festival in Hot Springs National Park, Arkansas, but I began to spend my off-hours listening obsessively to vintage recordings of Yiddish singers and researching what printed music resources I could find. Through my musician network, I was invited to sing with the Meshugga Klezmer Band for a Chanukah show at the Clinton Presidential Library in Little Rock in 2010, and then I was hooked. Since I had a lot of experience as an arts administrator, I decided to produce and direct a klezmer/Yiddish music show, "Oy Vey Cabaret," on the night of my 50th birthday in 2011, the fringe benefit of which was that none of my friends could throw me a surprise party.

How did you come to your cabaret persona Myrna Oy? What were some notable collaborations or performances you've done?

The name "Myrna Oy" was a gift from my then-colleague/now-partner Andy Muchin, host and producer of the public radio show "Sounds Jewish." While developing the "Oy Vey Cabaret," I created 'punny' cabaret names for all four of my fellow lead singers, and then Andy coined mine, which stuck.

Soon after that event, I moved back to my native California to care for my elderly parents. I used my move as an opportunity to experiment with solo performance formats I could adapt to a variety of small venues, as well as to work with established Yiddish song artists such as Jeanette Lewicki, and even to conduct two seasons of a Broadway-style Yiddish musical with the San Francisco Bay Area-based New Yiddish Theatre Ensemble.

What is the distinction between Yiddish theater music and klezmer?

In its original sense, klezmer refers to characteristic Eastern European Jewish folk music, played for weddings and other community occasions by small bands of ear-trained itinerant musicians. Yiddish theater music, which developed in late 19th century Europe, contained elements of klezmer, but its Jewish character comes mostly from its language and cultural themes. When both genres arrived in the New World on waves of late 19th and early 20th century immigration, they cross-pollinated with jazz and the Broadway musical, spawning a golden age of Yiddish theater music along New York City's Second Avenue.

Why did "Lena from Palesteena" inspire you so much? Also, can you talk about "Lena in Quarantina"?

The 1920 comic song "Lena from Palesteena" is a perfect example of klezmer's encounter with ragtime jazz. It is sung in 'Yinglish,' which is to say its lyrics are in English, but its style is Yiddish-inflected New Yorkese. Its central character is a vampy young woman who plays the concertina, a small squeezebox instrument with buttons where modern accordions have keys.

To accompany myself for my solo shows, I learned to play the concertina, so it was almost inevitable that "Lena" became a signature song for me. Perhaps also inevitably, pandemic isolation drove me to recast its lyrics and record it as "Lena in Quarantina," in which Lena uses her concertina to create social distance rather than to attract lovers.

How did you get involved with KlezCalifornia? What is your role there?

KlezCalifornia, a nonprofit organization dedicated to klezmer music and Yiddish culture, first came on my radar as I researched the San Francisco Bay Area klezmer community, preparatory to my return to California. As soon as I attended one of its workshops, I knew I had found my tribe. In the years since, I have worn a variety of KlezCalifornia organizational hats including showcase performer, stage manager, workshop administrator, board member, and, for the past six years, board chair.

I am so proud of this small but mighty nonprofit, whose "pandemic pivot" serves the global klezmer community through a continuing series of online workshop events.

Upcoming shows, current projects and future plans, etc.?

As is the case for all musicians around the world, my performance life has been completely disrupted by the pandemic. I have been a regular guest singer with the Victoria, BC band The Klezbians, with whom Andy and I also collaborated on a *Purimshpiel* musical play. This year, we successfully took our *Purimshpiel* online, but I hope to be able to participate in a cautious return to live performance soon.

Other comments?

Klezmer music and Yiddish song came from a culture that only survived through adaptability and resilience. I cannot imagine a more life-affirming gesture for our uncertain times than to make and share this art.

BEN ROSENBLUM

Ben Rosenblum is a jazz musician who plays accordion and piano in Ben Sutin's Klazz-Ma-Tazz band.

Why do you play klezmer?

    I was introduced to klezmer music by violinist Ben Sutin through his band Klazz-Ma-Tazz. We are both jazz trained musicians, but Ben wanted to explore the klezmer tradition more thoroughly, and asked if I'd be willing to learn and experiment with the music. As I've learned more about the music, I've come to feel that the time I spend with klezmer music deepens the connection I feel to my Jewish heritage.

    I did not grow up with klezmer music, but I have Jewish ancestry on both sides of my family, and something about the music clicks with something deep inside. Through klezmer music, I've also had opportunities to connect with the Jewish community in ways I would not have otherwise - for example, performing concerts for Holocaust survivors. While my musical interests take me to many places, I imagine klezmer music always having some role in my musical career.

Why do you think it has survived as an artform?

I think the melodies connect with me the most. Judaism is one of the oldest and richest cultures, and I think especially within the melodies of the various klezmer songs, you get a sense of how diverse the cultural influence has been on the Jewish tradition. This influence goes in both directions too – Jewish culture has influenced and been influenced by all the countries it has traveled through over the years. In klezmer you hear influences from Eastern Europe, the Middle East, the Balkans and Roma culture, but also Latin music through Ladino culture, Western Europe through German folk influence, and so much more.

In modern klezmer, you can continue to hear this cross-cultural blending continue in the mixture of klezmer with jazz, punk and many other genres. In these timeless melodies and the countless ways they are interpreted, you hear the history of the Jewish people, their diaspora and all the places where Jews have traveled and settled. I think it has survived precisely for this reason; because the music is so adaptable and is able to carry on its identity even while it assimilates the influences of so many other traditions.

What are some of your favorite songs and why? Include original compositions too.

I'll always be a fan of the most classic songs; pieces like "Der Heyser Bulgar," "Odessa Bulgarish" and "Tumbalalaika." They have been recorded by so many groups that the listener can always find something new in them with every recording.

PAVEL ROYTMAN

Cantor Pavel Roytman interprets prayer through song for his congregation in Wilmette, Illinois, and sings in the Maxwell Street Klezmer Band.

When did you start playing klezmer?

In Russia in 1991. I came to the US in 1994.

With your very early studies in classical music, how did you start studying and eventually playing klezmer?

First, let's define klezmer which is primarily instrumental music. However, it was influenced and paired up with Yiddish song early enough so today both are referred to as klezmer Jewish music, and this was something that identified me as a Jew in the former

USSR in the absence of religion. I heard it from my grandparents since the time I was a child and also in a form of the "gangster" song, or *chanson*. Finally, my dad, who taught me my first notes, grew up with the early Soviet Style Big Band music which was a reimagining of the Yiddish folk song genre into the big band style. This was a similar process to that of the integration of Yiddish song in America into the mainstream Broadway and popular music.

The Soviet Union did not encourage ethnic expressions en masse. There were two different Yiddish groups under the watchful eye of the KGB. The Jewish performers, sheet music and recordings were actually somewhat available but in a very limited way with the stamp of approval. Most (not all) of these songs were "doctored" to fit the Soviet narrative and the performers had to be "approved" just to be more accurate. When the October Revolution happened in 1917, everything became free. Jews became emancipated and Jewish theater really took off. Then when Stalin came there was pressure put on Jewish music and it went underground, which occurred through the end of the Soviet Union.

Until the collapse of the Soviet Union in 1987, Yiddish music was more or less underground. It was available in the form of pirated recordings in the US and Israel; in restaurant music, etc. There were official Yiddish bands in the USSR but they were more or less just for show.

The collapse of the Soviet Union happened at the time when I entered my last years of college and first years of conservatory, and I was eager to sing the new music in the atmosphere of relative freedom. All of a sudden, the Jewish community centers opened up and we got opportunities to sing Jewish music. I met a bunch of similar-minded friends and that is how this all started for me.

In the Klezmer Shpil Orchestra, did you know that your recording "Yiddish Songs" would become so beloved?

Even though we were not a world-renowned group at the time we made a name for ourselves in Scandinavia. In part it happened because Yiddish music was just coming back. We came to Finland to perform in 1992. Itzhak Perlman's recording "In the Fiddler's House" came out at around the same time and it was considered an example of the renewal. So we were in the right place at the right time. At that time klezmer had a revival in Sweden and Norway mostly by non-Jews, and many found Soviet Jews playing and singing Yiddish music as fresh and interesting

How does your spiritual life as a cantor inform your music?

I sing with klezmer bands, and klezmer has been intertwined with vocal music since its inception. In many instances it mocked traditional synagogue music and in others it borrowed from it. The process also went both ways. Klezmer music was always the music of the people and lifecycle events (like weddings). And I think it competed for attention with service music of the synagogue which was highbrow compared to klezmer. There were musical borrowings back and forth.

In addition, klezmer had many non-Jewish influences including gypsy music, for example. This made it more interesting and accessible to a wider audience. Interestingly enough, accessibility and simplicity are some of the qualities people look for in synagogue music today. This allows many to relate to the service.

The scales employed by klezmorim are often perceived as authentically Jewish and therefore suited more for traditional/conservative service than the Germanic Western service of the Reform synagogue.

For me, Yiddish and klezmer music are a personal way of expressing my Judaism. I grew up hearing and singing Yiddish and klezmer. This was my way of connecting to Judaism and obviously it is something that I can express more masterfully and in a more authentic way.

What in particular do you like about the music: the harmonies, melodies, chordal structure, etc.?

All of the above. It expresses who I am.

Now remember, klezmer/Yiddish is a distinctly Eastern/Western European genre. The Jewish community is not exclusively that (it never has been). So as far as the expression of Jewishness goes, it does so through Yiddish and klezmer primarily for the Ashkenazi Jews.

As an Ashkenazi Jew from Russia, I believe that Yiddish and klezmer are part of my identity. In a larger sense this music has a taste of tradition and it is easy to relate to (it is in many ways *the people's music*). Even though it has certain very unique Jewish features, it is full of borrowings from other cultures and musical and ethnic genres, and this truly makes a world music genre.

Do you have any favorite classic klezmer songs?

I love the songs of Yiddish theater especially from the 1930s and '40s. These are my favorite. Also, Russian Jewish gangster songs.

Is there a scene for klezmer in Wilmette? Is the scene opening up, post-COVID?

We performed several times during the summer. We had one concert with a live audience and the rest was streaming. I was involved in a bunch of virtual concerts all over the world from St. Petersburg in Russia to Mexico City.

There is a distinct Chicago style of klezmer that is infused with jazz and blues with a strong swing component, like from Benny Goodman, Ira Gershwin and Louis Armstrong. In fact, we're writing a show about it.

Other comments?

A word of gratitude to Lori Lippitz, Alex Koffman and the Maxwell Street Klezmer band for their friendship and partnership. Their distinct Chicago klezmer style is truly special and they have done an amazing job in preserving and promoting klezmer music around the world.

Also, a shout out to Russian-born Chicago klezmer musicians who, in spite of difficulties, continue to play and share their music with us.

"When I first heard the old klezmer recordings from New York and East Europe over 40 years ago, I was immediately attracted to the high level of musicianship and the expressiveness in a completely (to me) unfamiliar musical language. As I moved into scholarship and teaching, I discovered that my own great-grandfather had probably been a klezmer in Kiev in the late 19th and early 20th century, which made my involvement in this music even more meaningful to me. I feel blessed to have had a long career as a performer and recording artist on several continents and as founder and co-founder of groups such as Brave Old World, Rubin & Horowitz and the Joel Rubin Ensemble and to collaborate with so many great players along the way."

- Joel Rubin, University of Bern, Switzerland/Institute of Musicology

PETE RUSHEFSKY

Pete Rushefsky plays banjo and "tsimbl," is the Executive Director of the Center for Traditional Music and Dance, and is active in Yiddish New York. He is also the author of "The Essentials of Klezmer 5-String Banjo."

How did you learn about klezmer?

I grew up in Rochester, NY, playing blues (on guitar) and later got heavily into Irish music (on banjo). So I was always attracted to folk music on stringed instruments. I had Yiddish-speaking grandparents who were always singing, and our synagogue had a wonderful cantor, Sam Rosenbaum, who was a champion of traditional cantorial music.

What I heard of klezmer was horn- and clarinet-dominated, so it didn't interest me. My parents had an album of klezmer clarinetist Giora Feidman at home. But in the back of my mind, I imagined there must be some way to approach the music with stringed instruments, and started researching it.

A few things happened in the mid-1990s. I found a Balkan Arts cassette of Dave Tarras (the Balkan Arts Center, which produced the tape, later changed its name to Center for Traditional Music and Dance, the very organization I am now director of!). Additionally, I jammed a bit with a girlfriend's father, who had a klezmer band in Philadelphia. Soon after, I heard Andy Statman's amazing klezmer mandolin music, which gave me hope to find a way into this music as a string musician. This idea was cemented upon seeing Itzhak Perlman's PBS special, "In the Fiddler's House," which captivated me from the opening scene set in the old Krakow Jewish district of Kazimierz. The Perlman TV program was a wonderful introduction to klezmer as fiddle music, which I could totally relate to from my explorations of old-time American and Irish music. Additionally, it featured a number of amazing young musicians from leading contemporary klezmer bands such as Brave Old World, Klezmer Conservatory Band and The Klezmatics.

Soon after I learned about the tsimbl, the traditional hammered dulcimer of klezmer. Hearing Andy Statman's Jewish Klezmer Music album with Zev Feldman on tsimbl was truly a life-changing experience. And then I met tsimblist Josh Horowitz at KlezKamp in

1996. In the next year I went from imitating a tsimbl on my banjo to acquiring a tsimbl, and that started me on the path I've been on ever since.

Do you feel that klezmer reflects either a social, political, historical or spiritual sensibility?

All of the above. People come to klezmer and the wider Yiddish cultural scene in search of different things. For many in the scene, our work is about expanding Jewish (or in my case American-Jewish) identity into the realm of arts/culture/aesthetics, in opposition to historical currents of American Judaism which frame Judaism in purely religious terms. So the klezmer/Yiddish movement can be seen as part of reclaiming and inventing a more holistic idea of a distinctive peoplehood.

Why has it survived?

Klezmer is both an art and a functional practice. The music has an important place in Jewish communities as a soundtrack for weddings, bar mitzvahs and other community celebrations. It offers beautiful expressive potential with echoes of religious/spiritual music and a deeply rooted Yiddish sensibility. And there is a wonderful international and intergenerational community that has grown up around the revitalization of the music.

Musically, have you been aware of more or less interest in it in recent years?

I think klezmer in America hit a certain peak in the mid-1990s, largely thanks to Itzhak Perlman's involvement and the investments of major record labels in promoting recordings. There was almost a top-down nature to the growth. Pre-reunification Germany's interest in klezmer was also important to the music's international visibility.

Then the Perlman program ran its course, the recording industry collapsed and Germany cut back on cultural funding with the costly integration of East and West. Though what we do in the Yiddish scene has little to do with Israeli politics, in fact they frequently diverge, tensions in the Middle East have an impact on the wider public's appetite for expressions of Jewish culture in the diaspora.

Today, I think there is again a quiet swell of growing interest as a new generation of musicians explores the music. This time it's much more grassroots, propelled by a network of international festivals, workshops and social media.

What are some of your favorite klezmer songs?

Strictly speaking from a traditional viewpoint, klezmer is instrumental music, not vocal music. During the music's revival, it's become acceptable to include vocal music as a way of diversifying programs for concert audiences.

I'm a specialist in European klezmer... exploring how the music sounded before mass-immigration and the destruction brought by the 20th century. I love playing old melodies, but more generally, I love the older musical aesthetic, which can be used as a starting place to create new music. This string-based music is more aligned with other East European folk music as well as Western classical music.

Would you say that as a body of work, klezmer is open to all kinds of unusual instrumentation?

In one sense I am a player of an "unusual" instrument, the tsimbl (*cimbalom*). But tsimbl has been an important part of klezmer's sound since the 16th century. With any instrument, if you want to create a place in the music, you have to invest thousands of hours figuring it out if you're going to be taken seriously by connoisseurs. I tried to do it on a five-string banjo and even wrote a book about it, but ultimately, I found my time would be better spent on an instrument that already had an accepted niche.

Talk about the sense of community. Do you play it as part of an ensemble, and what is the audience's reaction to it?

I play in a myriad of ensembles, duos, solo programs, etc. Most of these configurations are assembled quickly for a particular gig. Though it's not a huge scene, I get to work with a number of different people, and that has helped me build a wider social network. It's now rarer to play for audiences that grew up with pre-revival klezmer as part of daily communal life, so today you seldom get to experience that wonderful musical mutual recognition with audience members who can sing along with you, know the dances and correct your Yiddish.

However, at least here in New York, there's now a slowly growing critical mass of folks who have studied the songs, dances and language at workshops, festivals or even universities, so ironically though the population of native speakers is rapidly declining (outside of the Hasidic community), we're seeing more younger audience members who are engaging with the music in a familiar way.

How does your work at the Center for Traditional Music involve the championing of klezmer?

The Center for Traditional Music and Dance (CTMD) was one of the major progenitors of the klezmer revival. The center's work with clarinetist Dave Tarras in the mid-1970s to early 1980s spearheaded the music's early revival on the East Coast. These were the first programs to employ the term "klezmer" as a musical genre in English.

CTMD has been the organizational home of Yiddish New York (YNY). Now in its sixth year, YNY is presented in New York City each December, and is the successor festival to KlezKamp which ran for 30 years in the Catskills. Additionally, CTMD produces programs, concerts, lectures, workshops and "Tantshoyz" dance parties year-round through our An-sky Institute for Jewish Culture which promotes and helps to revitalize the practice of instrumental klezmer, the accompanying Yiddish dance tradition and Yiddish folksong tradition.

Recently (even before COVID-19) we've been developing more online resources. Our Yiddish Song of the Week blog (www.yiddishsong.wordpress.com) is edited by folklorist Itzik Gottesman and receives tens of thousands of visits from all around the world each year. Our Stonehill Jewish Song Archive (www.stonehilljewishsongs.wordpress.com) disseminates an amazing collection of hundreds of Yiddish songs performed by Holocaust survivors in New York in 1948. Most recently, CTMD has built a website, Inside the Yiddish Folksong, dedicated to pedagogy and research (www.yiddishfolksong.com), and has been a partner in the Klezmer Institute's work to disseminate rare, historical klezmer manuscripts from Ukraine at https://klezmerinstitute.org/kmdmp/.

How was KlezKamp 2021?

Yiddish New York is an amazing intergenerational festival that I helped to found as part of a group of leading performers, scholars and cultural activists. It's a treasure chest of what's going on in contemporary Yiddish arts, scholarship and social justice. Over 500 people attended daytime workshops and thousands attended evening concerts, dance parties, theater and jam sessions. This year the festival was all online due to COVID-19, and while we hope to be back in person next December, the online festival allowed us to connect with audiences and artists internationally.

COOKIE SEGELSTEIN

Cookie Segelstein is the director and fiddler in Veretski Pass.

Do you recall when you first heard klezmer?

I actually grew up with the music without knowing it was called klezmer music. My parents are Holocaust survivors from the Carpathian Mountains in what is now Ukraine, and I was handed a fiddle at the age of five and expected to play the music that my father sang to me. So I would say that what my folks called "music from back home" was a mixture of klezmer music, local Ukrainian tunes, as well as Yiddish songs. So even though I began taking lessons at that age, with classical music, I was still trotted out at holidays and get-togethers and expected to play the music from Europe that my parents' friends, all Holocaust survivors, would recognize.

What was your first opportunity to perform klezmer?

When I went to KlezKamp for the first time in 1992, I realize that this revival consisted of a lot of the music that I grew up with. In most cases when I was younger, I was just playing for family. Any performances that I did were of classical music. I ended up getting a degree from Yale in viola, and playing in the New Haven Symphony and the chamber group Orchestra New England. Most of my performance life was with classical music. That is, until I had children. Once I had children, I realized I would have to tell them about not only a tragic history, but some of the cultural traditions that I grew up with. It was only then that I started to come back into this music.

In 1990, the principal flutist in the NHSO, Adrianne Greenbaum, was trying to put a group together to play for her son's bar mitzvah. She leaned forward and asked me if I played klezmer music. I said that I could play Jewish music, yes, and she put together a group for that function. That group, called The Klezical Tradition, played up and down the tri-state area (New York, Connecticut and New Jersey) for many years. At one point, for a few years it was my main income. We played weddings, bar mitzvahs, parties, funerals, concerts and really any kind of celebration. Since Adrianne and I were also classical musicians, we often would play trio sonatas for the cocktail hour and then full-out klezmer music for the reception.

I then started playing with some of the established New York musicians like Ken Maltz, Howie Leess, Ray Muziker and Pete Sokolow. Since I could play by ear as well as read, I got a lot of work. During the mid-90s though 2008, it was not uncommon for me to have three to four gigs a weekend. Let's just say I got to know the New Jersey Turnpike and the Long Island Expressway really well. I traveled with groups, as a sideman, going to Cape Cod, Las Vegas or Martha's Vineyard. This also with my work and classical music, playing weddings, bar mitzvahs as well as symphony concerts.

How did your classical training influence your playing – and understanding of – klezmer?

The good thing about having classical training is that I could harmonically and melodically analyze what I was playing. It helped me in deciding what kind of improvisations to make. Also, when I was listening to field recordings of fiddlers from the region of and near the birthplace of my folks, I could decipher small snippets to arrange in my own way. And in my own compositions, in the style of the music we play, I have a vocabulary and a way to develop my works. Plus of course, it doesn't hurt to have spent many hours practicing to develop technical skills.

When we teach classical players to stretch their skills and play by ear, I know where they're coming from. I actually really started out as an ear player. When

I was a freshman in college, I was playing a viola concerto in my lesson. My teacher looked at me and said, "You are not playing the music in front of you. I think you're playing this by ear." I swore up and down that no, I was actually reading the music in front of me. He smiled and said, "You're playing the version that's in the listening library downstairs. This is a different edition." He then told me that he was going to turn me into a good music reader, but that this would be a very painful year for me. He spent that year drilling me inside, reading. Yes, it was painful. But I became a very good sight reader! Now when I teach my students, I see that there are some that learn by ear, and some that learn by sight. For each of these styles of learning, I try to incorporate the other, to help students become much more versatile musicians.

Are there fewer opportunities for women in klezmer?

Traditionally and historically, klezmer musicians were men. Part of the reason was that Jewish women were not allowed to work as musicians. They were expected to keep the home and basically serve their husbands and God. But when the revival happened in the late 1970s, interestingly, it was very welcoming to women, gay and lesbian musicians.

But in many cases, people assume that the band leaders are men, so there would be times that we would be doing a sound check and sound technicians would approach one of the guys in our group and ask for their sound requirements. They would say, "Talk to her, she's the leader!" Also often with the press, whenever we have done a project, journalists will assume that the creative impetus is driven by one of the guys. I know many of us, men and women and non-binary musicians, are working to change that. But of course, our type of music is not the only type that suffers from the state of sexism, it's pretty much throughout the arts.

I just recently got together with a group of women to address this very issue, and we plan to form a *Bund* of women, non-binary and men to work together on holding festivals and venues accountable to reach for more equitable hiring practices. There are some, including KlezKanada and Yiddish New York, and the now defunct KlezKamp (which was the first Klezmer festival), that have been working to make that happen.

In my teaching, I have 24 private students that are interested in a mix of classical and folk music. I find that generally, when the girls make mistakes, they apologize. When the boys make mistakes, they say, "Dammit!" I want them all to say *dammit!* Therefore, part of the work of creating a more equitable workplace is to teach young women to have confidence both on stage and in getting work for themselves, and to facilitate workshops for young women to learn how to navigate the musical workplace.

When and why did you form Veretski Pass and what do you love about this ensemble?

I was hired to teach at a workshop in Albuquerque in 2002. I was asked to teach with the accordionist/

cimbalom player Joshua Horowitz and put on a concert with him. We found that we taught well together, and had a blast doing the concert together. He said that I should meet Stuart Brotman, and that we should think about making a CD. Thus, our trio was formed in 2002. What was wonderful about working with these two musicians, and still is, is that we have mutual respect and trust musically. We are all musical risk-takers. We operate with a healthy amount of heterophony, loving musical chaos, and never stifle each other. Stu and his wife are very good friends of ours, and Josh and I are married!

Talk about the common elements, musically, of the various types of music you play in VP. What is most distinctive about klezmer itself when compared with these genres?

We have a specific style in the music we play. We don't categorize each other in terms of melody, accompaniment or rhythm. There are times that we are all playing three different versions of the melody at the same time. We enjoy chaos, so heterophony really is part of our style. We play co-territorial music also, like Hutsul tunes, Polish and Ukrainian as well as Moldavian and Romanian melodies. We merge these with known klezmer tunes with abandon, and also write many compositions for our projects.

It's very hard to say what is distinctive about the klezmer melodies, because they are so infused with music of neighboring peoples. We always say that what makes something sound Jewish is the audience member to whom it sounds familiar. I know that's an academically sloppy thing to say, but it's very hard to pull out the Jewish elements of many of these tunes.

Talk about Budowitz and some of your favorite gigs.

I join Budowitz in 2006, and we did a couple of tours. My favorite was when we recorded our live double CD in Geneva and Zurich. Budowitz has not been very active in the last 10 years, sadly, as we are all geographically pretty spread out. And it is expensive to bring in a six-piece group with musicians coming from different corners of the world.

I toured with Veretski Pass much more, because we've been together for almost 20 years. Some of my favorite things on tour were the people that we have met along the way. I still keep in touch with many of these colleagues and presenters from all over the world.

How is your work in the different summer camps and organizations helping to pass the torch to young and emerging players?

We are a very dedicated teaching group. We are all experienced teachers, and have developed a system to teach the elements of klezmer music in small, digestible bits. What's wonderful is that some of the up-and-coming youngsters in this scene, and I mean musicians in their 30s now, were once students and play beautifully. It makes me really proud.

Is klezmer a good context in which to teach history, and give an example if possible?

Since klezmer music was a functional element of Jewish life in Eastern Europe, very important to Jewish weddings with rituals associated with parts of the music, it's a very good way to teach history. You learn about the importance of the wedding in Jewish life, bringing together of families and communities to make the Jewish population bigger. There are tunes for each part of these weddings, which of course lasted seven or eight days. There were tunes to escort guests into the celebratory area, there were tunes for the mothers-in-law, for the first dance of the bride, and inviting the ghost of dead parents to the weddings. Importantly, there were also melodies and styles to facilitate pre-wedding rituals like the seating of the bride and the unveiling of the bride.

The *badkhn* (BAD-chen) was a mixture of poet, entertainer and master of ceremonies leading these rituals. He would often sing to the bride in couplets, reminding her of the serious nature of her responsibilities, and often the lead violinist whose job it was to make her cry. There are many reasons for this, one of which is that the wedding was considered to be as serious as Yom Kippur, the Day of Atonement. It usually was not very hard to make her cry, as often she was meeting her husband-to-be for the first time at the unveiling which was before the wedding.

What inspires you when you compose klezmer?

The pressure of a new project. And then I really need a quiet place just to mess around with my violin. When I find a link that I like, I expand upon it. Some of my compositions that are four to five minutes long started out with six measures of music. It's the typical one thing leads to another!

Other comments?

One thing I want to say is that growing up, I hated this music. I was forced to play for the refugees, all survivors of the Holocaust. I would be trying it out, play some tunes from "back home," and they would cry. As a youngster, that sucked! So I turn to classical music as a rebellion. I switched from violin to viola because they didn't know what it was.

I was always drawn to music even as a very young child, so the fact that I went into it for a living was not a surprise to my family. But later on in my father's life (he died in 2000), I decided to interview him, basically to do the fieldwork right at his kitchen table. I wanted to know specifics about the way the music was played in Veretski. At first, he didn't want to talk to me about it, because he couldn't understand why I wanted information about such unrefined music. He said, "You're studying Bach and Mozart and Brahms. Why do you want to know about this peasant music?" But I persisted, and he finally started talking to me about musical life in his town. I would play him a melody, and he would say, "Not like that." Eventually, he would say, "Yes! Just like that!"

An interesting thing happened also. When I came back from KlezKamp in 1992, still not associating what I learned back home with the term "klezmer music," I played him a melody that I had learned from him as a child. But I put in a lot of ornaments, lots of slides and trills, to impress him. He put his hands over his ears and said, "What is all that noise!?" He said, "I can't hear the music, there's so much noise in it." So that gave me the idea that I would just play the way that I learned growing up. Much of the way that I play right now, although developed throughout the years with other influences from many hours of listening to recordings and Josh's fieldwork and that of Stu and other colleagues, harkens back to the teachings of my father.

ZISL SLEPOVITCH

Dr. D. Zisl Slepovitch, Ph.D. is a woodwind / keyboard player, conductor, composer and a Yiddish and music educator. On social media: @zislepovitch.

You play several instruments. Which did you start with, and which is your primary instrument today?

I started listening to the many records that we had at home when I was growing up, and to my mom and dad playing the piano and the guitar and singing, as gifted amateur musicians. Having majored in musicology and ethnomusicology later in life, I can't stress enough the important of listening (and participating) in music early in one's life. I tried to make sounds on my grandmother's piano that her father, a military clarinetist in the Russian czarist army, brought home to Mogilev, Belarus, after WWI. I remember those ivory keys and the beautifully carved wood. That piano became the first instrument I learned to play.

The story is somewhat funny. One beautiful morning when I was five, my dad asked me, "Do you want to join the music school [which was conveniently located a few blocks away from my regular 1—11 English school]?" Me: "Yes!" Dad: "What instrument would you like to learn?" Me: "Trumpet." Dad signs me up for the piano class. I still want to play the trumpet, and maybe I will someday, but I am sure grateful for dad's decision.

My luckiest moment at that school, Children's Music School No.3 in Minsk, was not the piano lessons. Those were beneficial, of course, and led me to develop my love for keyboard instruments as I later moved on to learn and perform on the organ and the harpsichord; and a lot of my freelance jobs in the United States when I moved here in 2008 were the rehearsal pianist and conductor-pianist for various theatrical productions in New York. But much more formational and life-determining for me was meeting my composition teacher, Valery Karetnikov, with whom I continued my studies later, when I went to high school, the National Music Lyceum (now College) at the Belarusian State Academy of Music.

Mr. Karetnikov taught me the basics of form and logic in music, and he suggested my parents buy me classical music records, which they did, a lot (and I listened, all the time). He was a philatelist like myself (and my dad), so sharing an extramusical passion helped me build an already steady bond and love for the subject. Also, I figure I was a natural improviser and a loved to write – texts and music, so a lot of composition course was learning the form, the orchestration, texture, melody – all those things — by going through a massive number of scores and records and quickly trying to reflect on them in whatever I could churn out myself.

In the 5th grade, as I was analyzing Tchaikovsky's Sixth Symphony score while listening to Mstislav Rostropovich conducting the National Symphony Orchestra, I suddenly realized that I wanted to become a conductor. I wanted to absorb and transcend all that beautiful music in the multitude of the orchestral and vocal timbres, on stage. Then I came up with an idea that I would probably need to learn an orchestral instrument, something in addition to the piano. While there was no oboe teacher in Music School No. 3, there was a clarinet teacher who agreed to teach me, from scratch. Clarinet happened to be a natural extension of my body. I immediately fell in love with it, even the terrible Soviet clarinet that the school had to lend, with keywork not properly functioning and me having little understanding of the whole wide beautiful woodwind world.

As soon as I covered the technical bases on the clarinet, in about a year or so, I had an amazing opportunity to immediately jump into performing and even touring, and also extensively arranging and composing for the mixed vocal-instrumental ensemble I was part of.

The primary tool of trade has been shifting all the time throughout the years, but I do believe I have been keeping a healthy balance between music scholarship (I got my Ph.D. in musicology in 2006), woodwinds, and keyboards, plus conducting, vocal coaching, composition, arrangement, consultancy, acting, and many auxiliary things. The multiple skills acquired over the years, adding to the Yiddish language and culture, played out to my great benefit in the long run, considering my immigration to America where I started from scratch as a freelancer (as opposed to my tenure position at the Belarusian State Academy of Music). I have learned more woodwinds, more keyboards, better conducting, better writing, everything I know about theater — and jazz, all those terrae incognitae.

What was your intro to klezmer?

My first introduction to the Eastern European Jewish instrumental music (now commonly called "klezmer") was a cassette of the Salomon Klezmorim duo that my dad brought me from the Netherlands when I was 15. I had just joined National Music Lyceum as a musicology major, and that record was a formational one. Clarinetist Marcel Salomon and accordionist Theo van Tool are great musicians, but that was not only about their musicianship, it was about the sense of music I had been deprived of, growing in the "internationalist" but essentially anti-Semitic USSR. My practical introduction to Jewish music, Yiddish and Hebrew songs, happened several years earlier, when I joined the Jewish youth ensemble *Simcha* in my hometown Minsk, originally named *Di grininke beymelekh* – The Little Green Trees.

When and why did you create your different ensembles (Litvakus, your Trio and others)? How would you describe the different material you perform in each group?

I had been playing with an instrumental group that I formed that was part of the mentioned Simcha Jewish Youth Ensemble: these were all my schoolmates, first from the Lyceum, and then predominantly from BSAM. I had arranged quite a few Yiddish and klezmer pieces both for the choir and orchestra, and the orchestra alone. I felt we were ready to go on our own, as a klezmer conservatory septet, in 2000, when I was about to graduate from BSAM.

We recorded our first CD as Minsker Kapelye klezmer septet, *A Fayerl far dem Hartsn (A Sparkle for The Heart)* in 2001, at BSAM, and set out on several tours, the highlight being the tour of Germany in the spring of 2003. For several reasons by the fall of 2004, we "downsized" to a trio, with me on the clarinet, folk flutes and vocals; Tatsiana Kukel on the Belarusian alto cimbalom; and Violetta Herman (nee Korenkova at the time) on the cello, later replaced by Hanna Kharchanka. I was excited to reconstruct that "old country / old time" feel, and also the feel of authentic, roots music of Belarus, which Jewish music was obviously part of, but a well-forgotten and never enough researched part. I was heavily influenced of the roots bands led by ethnomusicologists-performers, like Di Naye Kapelye led by Bob Cohen, an American expat in Hungary, or the fusion of the roots, classical and jazz in the klezmer supergroup Brave Old World with Alan Bern, Michael Alpert, Kurt Bjorling and Stu Brotman.

But then the Hungarian ethnomusicologists' group Muzsikás grabbed my attention and stole my heart. Their "The Lost Jewish Music of Transylvania" was constantly on my playlist. I knew that Belarusian culture, despite being suppressed by Russia / USSR for centuries, has its strong core, its great potential, and I also knew that the Jewish culture that thrived in Belarus (or Jewish Lithuania, to be more exact) for over 650 years, had a lot to share, if we could only find its traces. I think it was when we formed the Minsker Kapelye trio in 2004 I came to understanding that early / Baroque music, klezmer music, and improvised music (call it jazz or not) are in reality much closer than I was taught to think, especially in the modern world.

As a trio, Minsker Kapelye recorded two albums, both in Poland, and one of them in collaboration with Paul Brody's Sadawi, a klezmer-jazz band from Germany and the US. In general, meeting Paul Brody as well as David Krakauer and many others of the modern Yiddish / klezmer community led me to exploring not only the old klezmer repertoire, but new ways to make it your own creative language. I certainly learned bits of musical vocabularies that were new to me, which I think really opened me up and helped me be myself.

At that time, in 2004—5, I also co-produced two klezmer-jazz festivals in Minsk, Belarus, which were unheard of cultural events. The press and the audience alike were raging— in a good way. And I was happy, because I had that amazing opportunity to share with my home country something beautiful that I had just recently discovered in the world of music. I think it was then when I realized that I could transcend my passion for music, or art in general, to others, via my action — as a performer, producer, and scholar; that I had that kind of almost magical power — to ignite other people's hearts with the beauty that I couldn't get enough of.

In New York, I started the Litvakus band. Most of us met in the pit of the National Yiddish Theatre Folksbiene production of *Gimpl-Tam* (Gimpel the Fool), after I. B. Singer in the fall of 2008. It took us a while to figure out repertoire, style, but also the leading creative idea, what we were really trying to do. Following the release of our first full album, "Raysn: The Music of Jewish Belarus," in 2014, a critic called Litvakus "the acoustic Gogol Bordello," referring to a folk-punk émigré group. I used to call our style a shtetl disco, rock of the forests and marshes. Sure enough, it was much deeper than all those descriptions combined. It was about bringing many worlds together, many locations, periods, personal backgrounds that we had, and it all played well, I think, for the benefit of creating the unique sound and creative idea that Litvakus has formed over time. We would play old repertoire that I was fortunate to research in the archives of Russia and Belarus, I would write original pieces — both instrumental and vocal ones. It is easy to work with great, sensitive, highly skilled, intellectual musicians. It is really a privilege, and New York is certainly one place to find such musicians.

Zisl Slepovitch Trio, with Nadav Lev on the guitar and Dmitry Ishenko on the bass, was born as an irregular Friday night gig at Broadway Dive at 101st and Broadway. It was about the music we loved, you know, roots/traditional music of all sorts, early music, original pieces that I wrote specifically for that trio — basically improvised music based on anything. The latest theme we started focusing on was the music of the Grand Duchy of Lithuania, so Renaissance and early baroque music from my home neck of the woods that was long forgotten and found in the 1990's. Improvising on Renaissance music, with a mix of early and modern instruments, I think, represents our time and our place in history as modern musicians who happen to literally play everything with everyone, all over the world.

What sets klezmer apart from other traditional music throughout the world and why do you love it?

Jewish music from Eastern Europe, vocal and instrumental alike, carries the unique combination of the Mediterranean idiom found in many Jewish traditions across the globe, and the inimitable local flavor. This is a signature cocktail that I can drink and offer to others all the time, because it's so good.

Some of your favorite collaborations?

There were many, thankfully. One of the more formative collaborations happened to be with the wonderful trumpet player, band leader and composer

Paul Brody, with whom we recorded and did a short tour. I can't but name my mentor Michael Alpert whom I had invited to be part of my multimedia project, Traveling the Yiddishland, based on my fieldwork footage from Belarus. Outside of the groups that I lead, my longest collaboration has been with the National Yiddish Theatre Folksbiene. I have contributed to a good dozen of roles, and over 20 productions that we did together since 2008.

Since 2018, I have been a musician in residence at Yale University's Fortunoff Video Archive for Holocaust Testimonies. My job there is to research, curate, arrange (or, if need be, score) music, and produce records — the songs and poetry that survivors performed for the Archive. For some five years now, I have been playing with Dance Clarinets big band led by the notable reed player J.D. Parran, at Greenwich House Music School. Performed with a fantastic company of musicians, Dance Clarinets has been my introduction to the American orchestral jazz music, specifically that of St. Louis tradition, which I honestly had little to no idea about. We have done some interesting projects with Frank London and Hankus Netsky, both in musical theater and music.

A lot of encounters probably don't exactly count as collaborations, but they nevertheless have been memorable and inspirational to me: watching Itzhak Perlman play something I wrote was an unforgettable moment, sharing the stage with him, with Joshua Bell, Chita Rivera, Topol, being on a set with Daniel Craig, Liev Schreiber, working in a production directed by Joel

Grey doing something that he liked, and just being around many luminaries over these years, you know... I can't and won't ever take any of that for granted, coming from a more underprivileged group in one of the more underprivileged countries in the world. All these encounters, collaborations, stage-sharing, watching, playing, and listening experiences have been a much-needed gulp of fresh air.

What do you love about working in film and theater, especially as it helps expose audiences to klezmer?

I believe in a popular statement that a creative artist plays themselves all their life, trying to convey a set of ideas that are crystallized as central to them, but also that is happening in the process of learning — about the world, the people, their stories, and so on. When I had my first teaching practice in the 12th grade — I think I had to teach one of the Wagner's Ring operas to a group of 11th graders — one note that I got from my supervisor was that my lesson looked a bit like a talk show. While realizing that the note was rather a critique, I couldn't help feeling complimented. Being serious about your subject and putting on a show are not two contradictory modes in my mind, although I totally respect quiet conversation as a way of discussing deep and complex matters. Because I am a Jewish music (and other music— classical, improvised, etc.) scholar and performer, taking it to the film set allows me to contribute my expertise as a music historian, because you know, historical facts are so often being overlooked in film productions. Apparently, some people care about such things, even if there is a handful of them.

Bringing the Eastern European Jewish style to "Fiddler on the Roof" in Yiddish, a commercial off-Broadway production was not a mere poetic license, not a liberty for the sake of such. It worked together with the Yiddish script that took us back to the original language of Sholom-Aleichem's stories about Tevye the Dairyman. There were many elements in that production (which I am really proud of, on many levels) that all worked together, in system, towards that one goal of bringing authenticity of the roots culture to Broadway that often delivers a very different kind of aesthetic, let me put it this way. Of course, I am happy when a major production asks me to contribute klezmer music, something to which I have devoted all my professional life. It's not just that, but also the fact that I have devoted most of the past 13 years to theater, and I have learned a great deal of the way it functions, from many angles— production as such, fundraising, timeline, promotion, and so on. Understanding both sides make the ideas I am suggesting feasible for implementation on stage or set.

Upcoming projects?

Go back to being a working (in person) and traveling (beyond the internet) musician. But seriously, several recordings need to be done as we speak. I certainly acknowledge the temporal nature of my answers for the genre of book that might be read decades from now, but the question implied that, so here we go...

– Volume 3 of Songs from Testimonies in the Fortunoff Video Archive at Yale University: we had to postpone the recording due to the COVID-19 pandemic with Sasha Lurje and Zisl Slepovitch Ensemble. We all can't wait to reconvene from both sides of the Atlantic to create together again and lay these tracks.

– Zisl Slepovitch Trio's first record. We have been developing our program for a couple of years, trying to find our very own voice as a collective; and now when we did, the pandemic broke out. We now need to, again, reconvene from New York and Israel to have that done.

– This is more of a hope than a solid project, but yes, hopefully "Fiddler on the Roof" in Yiddish (*Fidler Afn Dakh*) national tour and perhaps some international trips as well, which was in the cards before the pandemic hit.

– A new album (or two) of my new Yiddish songs, both originals and arrangements, and contemporary classical compositions.

There are a couple more projects that are not as ready and I won't name them here, for now.

Other comments?

The klezmer musician cannot, does not, and has never historically been in a cultural bubble. Quite the opposite. From what I am observing, I would strongly encourage people who are interested in klezmer to find and listen to, transcribe and understand early through mid-20th century recordings. Abe Schwartz, Naftule Brandwein, Dave Tarras, Der Titunshnayder, American, Soviet, Polish, Romanian Jewish records from that era, field recordings by Kisselgof, Engel, Beregovski, Magid, and so on, and, no less importantly, find your community by way of learning and doing.

HAL SLIFER

Hal Slifer is the producer and radio host of Chagigah
Radio at WERS Radio, Boston, Massachusetts.

**You started off in radio and then veered into another
direction. Why did you decide to come on board at
WERS Radio?**

As a young boy I knew my career would be as a radio
DJ. I studied media at B.U. and upon graduation I spent
a few years as a DJ at various radio stations in New
England and eventually as a popular DJ at WGIR-FM in
Manchester, NH.

The pay of a DJ was not one to enjoy if I wanted to
get married and raise a family. I traded in my mic for a
video camera and started a successful video company. I

still kept in touch with all of my radio friends and after 20 years I sold my video company.

My first radio gig was in Berlin, NH, and my radio programmer was Jack Casey. As it turned out, Jack was now the general manager of WERS and needed someone for the Jewish music program called" Chagigah" [Hebrew for "voluntary sacrifices."] Jack offered me that job once I sold my video company.

I changed the style and flavor of Chagigah and after a few months was also offered a job as radio host for the Triple A music format that WERS played on weekdays.

When did your interest in Jewish music begin and why do you enjoy it? Does it help to inform people about their culture, heritage and faith?

I came from a contemporary religious family growing up. We went to services on the weekends yet during the week we were not religious. My mom sang in a Jewish choir and my dad enjoyed buying also sorts of albums from show music to the Barry Sisters. I was more into rock and roll music growing up.

I went to a Jewish camp from age 7 to age 18 and although the camp was a co-ed sports camp they did get involved with Jewish culture, music and traditions, and I enjoyed that.

I always had a great feeling about being Jewish and when I was offered the position to change the format of Chagigah, I made it into a musical program that included the memories of growing up Jewish. We don't get into religion on Chagigah Radio. We get into the sweet memories and traditions of growing up Jewish, and music is the common denominator.

How important is klezmer in your daily lineup?

Since we are the only contemporary Jewish music program in Boston and streaming worldwide, I need to satisfy the many different styles of music for our large audience.

There are a few other programs that play Jewish music in Boston, yet none of these programs make the ratings or have a large audience as Chagigah Radio does.

We play everything, as long as the tune is by a Jewish singer or at least composed by a Jewish songwriter. We can go from the music of Leonard Cohen to Benny Friedman to Erik Einstein and David Broza to klezmer by Giora Feidman followed by a song sung in Hebrew that is a Beatles cover tune, and follow that up by playing The Barry Sisters and Ezekiel's Wheels Klezmer Band.

Klezmer music makes up about 20-30% of our music playlist on any Sunday's program. Many times, a klezmer tune can be a Yiddish tune.

What klezmer artists do you regularly feature, and what new/emerging artists?

We play new and old klezmer. Our more popular tunes are by The Klezmer Conservatory Band with such tunes as the Leonard Cohen classic "Dance Me to The End of Love" or "Belz, Mayn Shtetele Belz," Ezekiel's

Wheels Klezmer band with "Sheyn Vi Livone" or The Klezmatics with "Kats Un Moyz." Yale Strom and Hot Pstromi are also favorites of our audience.

We also reach back to the history of klezmer music with music by Max Epstein, Sid Beckerman, Giora Feidman, Andy Statman and Mickey Katz.

Do you feel the interest in klezmer has increased, decreased or stayed the same since you are in radio?

Good question. Klezmer groups did tour shuls, schools and Jewish organizations before the pandemic and hopefully post-pandemic these groups are continuing to tour.

There have been klezmer revivals in each of the decades from the 40s through the current times. Klezmer is a niche audience of lovers of this music and this style of music has been morphed into the American music scene for many years.

Some of your own favorite artists and songs of the klezmer world?

I enjoy the music of Andy Statman, Giora Feidman, Ezekiel's Wheels Klezmer Band, Klezmer Conservative Band, Mickey Katz, Alicia Svigals, The German Klezmer Allstars, Kapelye, The Village Stompers, Benny Goodman Orchestra, Barcelona Gypsy Band, Budapest Klezmer Band and Maxwell Street Klezmer Band, among many others.

Other comments?

I would love to see klezmer music enjoyed by a new and younger audience. In Boston, NYC and the West Coast, I find that klezmer is thriving.

MARK SLOBIN

Mark Slobin is an ethnomusicologist, Winslow-Kaplan Professor of Music Emeritus at Wesleyan University, and the author of "Motor City Music: A Detroiter Looks Back" and "Fiddler on the Move – Exploring the Klezmer World."

What are the specific qualities of klezmer that you are drawn to?

It's not specific. It's the overall blend of soul and skill.

Although klezmer is written, played and enjoyed by secular individuals as well as religious individuals, there are similarities with Jewish music.

How does modern klezmer differentiate itself from the body of religious music that it, in part, originated from?

"Modern klezmer" has so many pathways now you can't generalize; even in the 1980s there were differing individual tastes and trends, but on the whole, there's less of an interest in "differentiation" and more of an interest in border-crossing, even with "religious" repertoires, musicians, and audiences. But "religious" is a bad word – Judaism was an entire cultural package that included all kinds of verbal/musical/artistic expression that flowed from a general aesthetic into different genre channels: liturgical, paraliturgical, folk, instrumental...

Experts talk about the klezmer revival in the 1970s/80s. What do you think contributed to a shift or development in the genre?

"Revival" is a technical term now in ethnomusicology and fits its earliest phase, but very quickly it went into "post-revival" and now beyond that as new voices claimed their space and you could see a process of constant building out from the revival foundations, adding wings, porches, tool sheds, whatever.

What is your impression of the body of work by Moshe Beregovski and what have his writings contributed to our understanding of klezmer?

Beregovski was a massively important figure in Jewish music studies. He deserves to be known beyond "Jewish."

In a phrase, it's his combination of scrupulous scholarship with open-minded theoretical thinking.

What are your hopes for klezmer as an artform today?

Don't have an agenda. It's being written every day by the newest generation, who are both faithful to their mentors and eager to blaze new trails. I look forward to the results.

ALICIA SVIGALS

Alicia Svigals is a klezmer violinist and a founder of the Grammy-winning group The Klezmatics.

How did you learn about klezmer?

When I was a teenager, my father worked in the New York City public schools and he was the supervisor of the arts program in East Harlem. He hired young artists, one of whom was Barbara Statman, who is married to Andy Statman, a great clarinetist and one of the first klezmer revivalists. Andy and Barbara visited our home and Andy, who was also a bluegrass mandolinist, taught me to play the blues. He invited us to his now-legendary Town Hall klezmer concert in New York City in 1979, which he gave with his musical partner, tsimbl player Zev Feldman. It was absolutely riveting! That was my first experience with klezmer.

I loved all kinds of ethnic music from when I was young. I took a year off college to hitchhike around Europe and busk, and I met and played with traditional musicians from all different cultures who were also defying cultural homogenization to be creators and active participants in locally sourced music. When I returned to college, I switched my major from neuroscience to ethnomusicology. It was a brand-new department and I was its first undergraduate. There was a grad student there working on the klezmer revival, interviewing another revival founding father, and she rekindled my interest in the genre. When I graduated college and was playing music full-time in NYC, I came across a classified ad in the Village Voice looking for musicians to form a klezmer band. That's how The Klezmatics were formed. I was one of the founders, and was a leader of the band for 17 years. I left the band in 2001.

Do you feel that klezmer reflects a social, political or spiritual sensibility?

Yes. For me, I express my Jewishness through music, much more than through religious observance.

I always felt that when we were playing it and the revival was new, the mission was to give secular Jews back our own musical traditions in the same way that there were living, thriving musical traditions in, say, the Irish and Greek communities in the US. My model was Greek music because I had a job after college playing in a Greek nightclub in Astoria, Queens, and it was a very happening scene, which I loved.

I became obsessed with the Greek fiddle style. I was really struck by how they had their own multigenerational musical culture which they were much more interested in than generic pop music. I thought, wow, we should have that too. My idea was not to approach klezmer as a museum piece, but to keep it going and bring in contemporary influences. That's what The Klezmatics were doing, bringing in all our other musical interests – rock, jazz, etc. I wrote one hip hop-like arrangement.

Why do you think it's survived?

It's great music. That's always going to be the bottom line. It's something that moves people and makes them want to dance, want to cry. Good art always survives and breaks through the other stuff. The music is complex, interesting and moving. and has a connection to something broader and deeper. And klezmer and the larger Yiddishist scene around it offers a kind of home for a lot of Jewish listeners and players who may not feel they have one in other Jewish settings (synagogue, Zionism, etc.).

What are some of your favorite songs?

All the compositions of Naftule Brandwein, an iconic klezmer clarinetist, who went beyond simple folk chord progressions. One of them is called "Naftule Plays for the Rabbi" which is a sophisticated piece of music.

Also, I like an American klezmer tune from the 1940s which was written on the chord changes of Charlie Parker's "Ornithology," called "Der Feter Max's Bulgar," recorded by the Sam Musiker Orchestra. And there's a series of tunes called "Romanian Fantasies" by klezmer fiddler Joseph Smolinski that I find haunting and beautiful.

Talk about the sense of community in playing, even with the online streaming model during the pandemic?

There's been a good response to Zoom concerts but it's not the same as in person. It's interesting from a performer's point of view. Sitting in the dining room makes it very intimate; it doesn't even feel like I'm performing, which has its pros and cons.

What new projects have you worked on recently?

The past couple of years I've been writing scores for silent films, which I then perform live during screenings: the *Yellow Ticket* with pianist Marilyn Lerner, the *Ancient Law* and *City Without Jews*, co-written, recorded and performed live with pianist Donald Sosin. Our latest score is the soon-to-be-released *Man Without a World*. My favorite shows have been at some of those big, old 19th century theaters with loges and columns that hold over a thousand people and have a pit for the orchestra.

And it was exciting to play at Lincoln Center in New York at the Walter Reade Theater. I recently wrote and recorded solo violin scores in more of a classical violin style for a compilation of early silent films called "Cinema's First Nasty Women" to be released in 2022.

ELEONORE WEILL

Éléonore Weill *performs in the klezmer bands Tsibele (and is also a founder member), Midwood, and Fada; and in the Joey Weisenberg Hadar ensemble.*

Was your initial attraction to klezmer because you grew up listening to it, or did your musical or spiritual exploration bring you there?

I grew up in a village in Southern France (near Toulouse). My father is a musician. He performs in a variety of musical traditions like Occitane, Persian, Italian and North African. My mother is from a French-Jewish artistic family (my maternal grandfather was a photographer who worked for the Yiddish Puppet Theater in Paris and collaborated with Marcel Marceau, among many others). So traditional music was omnipresent in our family life.

Once a month, our village was visited by the "MusiBus," a music library on wheels that allowed you to check out three CDs each month. So at some point when I was young, we checked out a couple of klezmer CDs.

Later on, when I was 14, a great tragedy happened. Our house burned down and we were forced to find a new home. My parents were given a very small apartment in the village, and so I ended up moving in with my best friend Lolla's family in a small city nearby called Albi. Lolla is also very musical, and so now that I was separated from my parents, I started listening to a lot of klezmer and we went to live shows together. Klezmer became a kind of home for me connecting me to the traditional music of my father and my mother's strong Jewish heritage.

At age 21, I had graduated from a conservatory and university in Toulouse and moved to Paris to study ethnomusicology at the Sorbonne, where I could focus on klezmer and Yiddish songs. I began to study klezmer with a pianist, Denis Cuniot, who introduced me to many of the klezmer musicians in the capital. That is also when I started to play in several klezmer bands and jams.

Do you find the music social, political, historical or spiritual?

Growing up in rural France with a Jewish last name, I always had to explain that I wasn't Israeli. Yiddish culture provided a way to affirm my Jewish identity that was distinct from modern Israeli culture.

Klezmer is a music that has no national borders, and in that way is subversive. It's not attached to any nation. It's from a time before these borders. It's diasporic, like the Jewish people...and the music reflects all the different places Jews were living. Jewish musicians were influenced by Roma, Moldavian, Romanian, Turkish, Hungarian, Greek, Ukrainian and Polish musicians and vice versa. Klezmer integrates musical ideas from these cultures and combines them with music of the synagogue and other spiritual and secular traditions. In many ways my own identity mirrors the multicultural mix embodied in klezmer. I wear it like the multicolored mosaic of the harlequin's costume.

I have a great conviction in the power of Yiddish music to create change. There are entire genres of Yiddish songs with social justice and resistance themes. Songs from a hundred years ago give voice to many of the same issues we face today: life under capitalism, tyranny and heteropatriarchy. For example, I sing and have recorded with my band Tsibele the song "Tsvelef a Zeyger" ("*12 O'Clock*"), which tells a tragic story of a man's violence on a woman. She is murdered by a suitor after she tells him that her mother does not approve of their relationship.

Another example is the song "Dem Nayntn Yanuar" (*"The Ninth of January"*), a musical setting I composed using lyrics collected by Moshe Beregovski in the 1930s during one of his musical expeditions through Ukraine. I also sing it in Tsibele's album "In Droysn iz Finster."

The song is really a call to action against the tyranny of capitalism and government. Its message of anti-incarceration has particular resonance in today's cultural climate.

Why do you play it today?

First of all, I love it.

As I write this, I am being displaced once again from a home (I'm in the process of finding a new apartment). Yiddish music provides sustenance and social connection-- an anchor in my life. The Yiddish arts community has become my family in my new life in America. And it's just so fun. The more I explore the music and culture, I continue to be amazed by the richness of Yiddish culture. It allows me to express my contemporary feelings, struggles and beliefs with reference to my cultural roots and share with others that can relate to those too.

My strongest desire and intention playing klezmer and singing in Yiddish is making people dance, help them forget for a bit their daily struggles, sharing some joy, love, strength to resist and fight for a better world for all.

What are the variations in the genre?

Klezmer and Yiddish songs are distinct though related music. Klezmer is traditionally an instrumental music, centered around communal celebrations such as weddings. Yiddish songs have a diverse repertoire including ballads, lullabies, table songs, children's songs, love songs, and songs of protest/resistance. There are entire genres of religious and spiritual songs including *nigunim* (wordless melodies) and songs for the Sabbath and other festivals. And I am probably forgetting some other genres!

What are the elements that resonate the most with you: the melodies, harmonies, rhythm...?

I have a particular interest in klezmer melodies, and the space they provide for improvisation, including melodic variation and ornamentation. Sometimes the tunes explore a mode in intricate and subtle ways, like the stitching of an embroidery.

Are there techniques specific to the genre you've had to learn?

There are ornaments (*dreydlekh*) particularly characteristic of klezmer. The most famous is the "krekhts," in which the instrumentalist makes and imitates a crying sigh, also called 'sanglot' or 'flagolet' in the French early music world. There are also a number of specific rhythms that underpin particular dance genres such as *bulgar* and *zhok*.

What are some of your favorite songs and why?

The "Romanian Fantasies" recorded on 78s by the violinist Solinski with a tsimbl player always have a special place in my heart. These melodies transport me to a special place of extreme beauty and calmness. I love the movement of the tsimbl accompaniment, conjuring images of a long ride in a horse-drawn carriage in Romania.

"Oy Dortn" is one of my all-time favorite Yiddish songs. It is a lullaby about love, a powerful expression of longing for a loved one who is across the ocean. Obviously, this has particular resonance for me, as an immigrant and during the pandemic.

MICHAEL WINOGRAD

Michael Winograd is a clarinetist and composer whose CDs include "Storm Game," "Kosher Style," "Tarras Band Plays Again" and "Sandaraa."

Why the clarinet?

I started out as a kid on sax and started klezmer as a young teenager. I went to a master class in New York City by David Krakauer who told me I should buy a clarinet. It spoke to me early on.

Why klezmer?

The moment I heard the stuff I was pretty drawn in musically. I was around 14. Growing up around NYC, I heard a lot of the best klezmer musicians experimenting with the music and that had a profound effect on me early on. A friend of mine had been attending KlezKamp, where his mother taught folklore, so I tagged along with him one winter and I was hooked. There I was exposed to the music in the larger context of Yiddish culture.

One of KlezKamp's great strengths was its multi-generational participation. For example, my first teacher there, Sid Beckerman, was in his 80s at the time, and it was so cool to be a 14-year-old studying with him. At the time I took for granted how special that was, and only years later did I truly come to appreciate that experience.

What was your first public performance like?

I had a little klezmer band at age 15 I had put together with a guitarist and trombonist. We played at the opening of a film called "Left Luggage" with Isabella Rossellini and Topol. The movie opened in Long Island where I grew up, at a theater in Huntington. I was referred to the gig by my teacher at the time, Matt Darriau of The Klezmatics. I had started studying with him and he hooked me up with this first gig.

To devote a band to Dave Tarras's work, what drove that decision and what is it about his catalogue that you are drawn to?

It's been a really fun project to be a part of. Dave Tarras's first recordings were in 1926 and the last was in 1978 so his work spans many decades. His style and persona evolved tremendously in that time. His repertoire also broadened with the growing popularity of Yiddish theater and radio. As a performer more comfortable with Western styles and good reading chops, Tarras was first call for these types of recordings unlike some of his contemporaries like Naftule Brandwein.

What's particularly rewarding about playing with Tarras Band is the opportunity to work with pianist Pete Sokolow, who worked with Tarras for decades. As a band we've made two records. The first was all Tarras material and on the second we included repertoire from other artists such as Brandwein and Sam Musiker. I look forward to getting this band back to work once live shows return.

You play in other ensembles. Talk about the different dynamics that can occur due to instrumentation, styles, etc.

In 2019 I put out "Kosher Style" with my band, Michael Winograd and the Honorable Mentshn, which, similar to Tarras Band, takes inspiration from the great klezmer recordings of the late 1950s. Following this time, the klezmer recording business went into hibernation for 20 years or so, but not before a series of five or six of my favorite records were released. A storm before the calm, if you will. I love these records specifically for their sound and production. It was the era of hi-fidelity recording, and it's a joy to listen to these LPs.

Albums like "The Dukes of Freilachland" by the Epstein Brothers and "The Happy People" from Danny Rubenstein are among my favorites, but the one that has had the most impact for me is "Tanz" featuring Tarras and his son-in-law, the great clarinetist Sam Musiker. Musiker split his time as a klezmer and jazz musician, most prominently a member of the Gene Krupa Band.

"Tanz," a record conceived and produced by Sam, is a perfect balance of high-energy dance numbers with lush, almost cinematically arranged numbers. In many ways "Kosher Style" was a direct reaction to "Tanz."

How do you compose when you start a song?

I often start with a source that already exists or I hear something in a record that I take a flavor from and build on that flavor. I write both at the piano and the clarinet. When I write from piano, it often starts at a more harmonic and chordal place; even a contrapuntal place. On the clarinet it's a more melodic and patternistic place.

What are audience reactions to klezmer today?

Klezmer music does have a dedicated fan base. Though small, this international audience is great to connect with while touring internationally. Is it growing? I'm not sure about that. Often it feels like it's pretty stagnant and at times that's not the most optimistic feeling. However, having this loyal audience during the pandemic has been a lifeline for many of us. All this to say that klezmer musicians, like all other musicians, are at the mercy of the music business in general. No surprise that it hasn't been getting easier in the last few years.

But let's see how the post-pandemic world is. I hope following this period that the value of live music and arts will come back even stronger.

What did you do during the lockdown and what are you doing now?

The Honorable Mentshn were touring in Europe as the pandemic hit last March and we had to turn around and head back home. It was unfortunate as we were just firing up the touring cycle for "Kosher Style." But after the first few weeks in lockdown, I got back to a more normal routine of practicing and writing, and out of that a new recording is in the works. Hopefully that will lead to another tour sometime soon.

I'm also the artistic director of KlezKanada, the yearly gathering and celebration of Yiddish music and culture. Generally, KlezKanada takes place at the end of August, just outside Montreal in the Laurentian Mountains. We realized last March we'd have to transition to a digital format. This transition took a major effort from our team, but out of it grew a truly great and rewarding virtual program.

I also got to work on a film score last winter. And while we originally had planned to have an in-person recording session for the score with musicians on both coasts of the US, we had to record remotely from our homes. While some of us have been recording from home for years, for some of the musicians this was the first time. A real learning curve and technical challenge! But very fun, and we are all looking forward to the film's release!

Debbie Burke

"Klezmer is like New Orleans Jazz. It's specific to Europe and has a unique set of musical modes. Consider the Doina, used in the intro of many songs. Generally a sad feeling, but then a burst of joy when the main theme comes in fast. No other genre does this so effectively."

- Keith Wolzinger, Los Angeles, CA
KlezmerPodcast

DEBBY YAFFE

Debby Yaffe plays rhythm guitar in The Klezbians and is based in Victoria, British Columbia.

Was your initial attraction to klezmer because you grew up listening to it, or did your musical or spiritual exploration bring you there?

It grew out of Jewish feminist celebrations.

When were you first exposed to klezmer?

I probably heard some of it all my life without thinking about it. I grew up not living in a Jewish environment and I wasn't that interested.

For me, klezmer came pretty late in life. I got into it in my 40s. I grew up playing guitar folk music in the '50s by ear. In the 1970s I was living in England, which is very Christian, culturally.

In the 1980s in Victoria, BC, I got connected to Jewish feminism, and eventually to klezmer.

Why do you think as an artform that it has survived?

They're easily portable instruments; can function on a private as well as public level; great good-time music for simchas; fusion with gypsy, jazz, swing makes it versatile; all those European Jews making it to New York City gave it a big boost.

Who are the musicians in the Klezbians?

There are nine of us. Three clarinets, two guitars, one accordion, one cello, and one sax, plus Sue, who can play trumpet, trombone, drums, banjolele, and a few other instruments, depending on what we need. Four of us are Jewish. We began with my partner playing "Dayenu" on accordion at our Jewish lesbian seders and gradually added instruments as more women were drawn in.

Normally we play every week, but not during COVID. We played all last summer outside and inside till about December. We'd play on the sidewalk and people driving by waved and clapped. There are some Yiddish speakers in town where we live, so if you sing, they sing along and they're so thrilled. My reading of music has improved. Even though I play chords rather than notes, I have to follow along.

Why do you play it today?

It's a lot of fun, part of my Jewish lesbian community celebrations and a great uplift to my spirit. Feels good to work towards performance goals. And it connects me to my partner, who died a few years ago.

Your favorite songs?

I like the fast and zippy ones. I love that so many of the melodies are happy tunes in minor keys. That feels quintessentially Jewish. Some of my favorite songs:

Der Rebbe Elimelech - We don't actually play it, I learned it elsewhere, but I love it because it's fun and lively.
Eileh Chamda Libi - We learned it for my granddaughter's bat mitzvah and it's great – a lively, pretty tune.
Abi Gezunt - We learned it from someone for a fundraiser for the synagogue's social welfare committee; I love the tune.
Bei Mir Bistu Sheyn - Gorgeous schmaltz.
Happy Nigun - Lively and fun.
A Nacht in Gan Eydn - You can do so many different things with it.
Odessa Bulgar #3 - I love the chord progressions.
The Rabbi's Hornpipe - It's fun and lively. We play it as a tribute to our heimische rebbe.

Why do you like playing klezmer as part of an ensemble, and what draws the community to it?

We don't play for money, just for fun (plus food and drink). We've played at weddings, parties, opening festivities at the local Jewish Film Festival, life celebrations, fundraisers for good causes, outside care homes during COVID, etc. and even though we are strictly amateurs, people respond so positively to our high-energy performances, it's great fun.

We recorded videos for my granddaughter's bat mitzvah. We once played in a bar in front of a bunch of super-cool types and by gum, they shut up and listened when we played.

I love participating in Jewish culture without having to do anything "religious." At one performance, someone told me they were thrilled to be able to do something in public as queer Jews. I love that we have raised money to bring in refugees, to help elect a progressive candidate for City Council, etc. because our music makes people feel expansive.

I don't get much pleasure from playing by myself, but playing music with other people is fabulous. So energizing. And we are very bonded. We've been through serious illness, deaths, various traumas and some triumphs together.

FINAL NOTE

Music is living, breathing, as organic as the trees and the fish. It is not meant to be placed on a wall in a museum. The roots of it – in particular, of klezmer – and the reasons for it coming about need to be understood, but the path it takes with today's musicians is not containable. Like a melon split open, klezmer is up for anybody to taste. Why have I included contemporary musicians whose roots may or may not have been steeped in the traditional and whose melodies and harmonies might not match with those of the past? It's because we need to respect it as a growing artform. Today's riffs and rhythms might not sound like our ancestors' klezmer. From where I stand, any musician has a right to this music, regardless of one's country of origin or genesis of faith. We can all take a bite and make it our own.

ACKNOWLEDGMENTS

Besides all the interviewees in this book who were extremely generous in doling out their time and perspective, I'd like to thank the readers and interviewees of my jazz blog. Without them, I would not have this amazingly diverse platform in which to talk about music. A special thanks to Jeff Rushefsky for his lovely foreword, Donna Lynn Photography for the retouching job on Grandma Sarah's photo and my bio photo, my ridiculously talented cover designer Charlie Coatney who's done his magic once again, and for the family and friends who continue to believe in me as I write from the heart.

PHOTO CREDITS

Phil Alexander c. David L. Hone
Robert Beck c. Tim Hakvoort
Debbie Burke (BIO) c. Donna Lynn/Rare Quality Talent
Glenn Dickson c. Matt Samolis
Oran Etkin c. John Abbott
Susi Evans c. Mart Photography
Richard Fay c. Tony Ioannides
Irith Gabriely c. Hannelore Anthes
Steven Greenman c. Pawel Mazur
Jim Guttman c. Randy J. Goodman
Curtis Hasselbring c. Caroline Mardok
David Krakauer c. GMD
Aaron Kula c. Jeff Tholl
Philippe Laye c. Cecile Aubry

Lori Lippitz c. David Sutton Studios

Alexandre Litwak c. Michel Bonnet

Allison and Wayne Marks provided by the Marks; book image c. Green Bean Books

Nami Melumad c. Roy Zafrani

Hankus Netsky courtesy of KlezKanada

Laura Rosenberg c. Andy Muchin

Ben Rosenblum c. CK Photography

Pavel Roytman c. Vitaly Kuznetzov

Pete Rushefsky c. Bob Blacksberg

Cookie Segelstein c. Lloyd Wold

Zisl Slepovitch c. Anya Roz

Hal Slifer c. Studio Eleven

Mark Slobin c. Manny Parks

Alicia Svigals c. Thierry Arsenault

Eleonore Weill c. Avia Moore

Michael Winograd c. Lloyd Wolf

Debby Yaffe c. Kath Farris

ABOUT THE AUTHOR

Debbie Burke is the author of "Icarus Flies Home," "Tasty Jazz Jams for Our Times" (Vol. 1 and Vol. 2), "Glissando – A story of love, lust and jazz," "The Poconos in B Flat" and "Music in the Scriptures." Her internationally acclaimed and geographically diverse jazz blog at debbieburkeauthor.com covers artists around the world from many different subgenres of jazz. She is an award-winning editor and ghostwriter, and the founder of Queen Esther Publishing LLC, a professional editing and author coaching firm.

Brooklyn-born, she has lived in six different states in the eastern half of the US but most of all loves being near the ocean. When she isn't writing, she's learning new licks on the sax.

Made in the USA
Middletown, DE
14 August 2021